# EXCEPTIONAL HOMES

THE CLASSIC STYLE OF RALF SCHMITZ, EST. 1864

# EXCEPTIONAL HOMES

THE CLASSIC STYLE OF RALF SCHMITZ, EST. 1864

RS

# INHALTSVERZEICHNIS

RS

# TABLE OF CONTENTS

RS

# EISENZAHN 1, BERLIN

BEIM BERÜHMTEN *KURFÜRSTENDAMM* ENTSTAND
IM KLASSISCHEN STILKANON DIESES *WOHNENSEMBLE*:
AUSSERGEWÖHNLICH, *NOBEL UND ZEITLOS*

*MAJESTIC, TIMELESS* AND REFINED, THIS NEW-BUILD
OFF THE FAMOUS *KURFÜRSTENDAMM* TAKES ITS
CUE FROM CLASSICAL ARCHITECTURAL TRADITIONS

FOTOS TODD EBERLE, GREGOR HOHENBERG, ANDREAS GEHRKE, SEBASTIAN TREESE    TEXT BETTINA SCHNEUER

*Noblesse, neu definiert: Der Bau mit zwölf
Wohnungen ist inspiriert vom Flair Pariser
Boulevards und eine Hommage an die
großbürgerliche Wohnkultur des Berliner Westens*

*Luxury living redefined: this twelve-unit building
references charming Parisian boulevards
and also pays tribute to the grand apartments
of old West Berlin's upper class*

*Lobby und Loggia zum Garten wurden exklusiv von Bottega Veneta ausgestattet; in der Mitte der ikonische Bibliotheks-tisch des italienischen Luxus-Labels*

*Lobby and garden loggia were exclusively furnished by Bottega Veneta; in the centre is the Italian label's iconic library table*

*„Bottega Veneta gestaltete exklusiv die großzügige Lobby und die Musterwohnung"*

*"The show home and impressive lobby feature exclusive decor by Bottega Veneta"*

*Durch die Ankleide aus Eiche, deren raffinierte Elemente RALF SCHMITZ entwarf, geht es in den Masterbedroom*

*Fitted out in oak, the dressing room off the master bedroom features smart RALF SCHMITZ-designed wardrobes*

*Kleines Arbeitsmöbel in typischer Lederbespannung samt Intrecciato-Regiestuhl im Schlafzimmer*

*Signature leather accents, including an intrecciato director's chair, grace the bedroom's mini workspace*

„*Creative Director Tomas Maier wählte Möbel, Textilien und Accessoires aus*"

"*Bottega Veneta creative director Tomas Maier chose the furniture, textiles and accessories*"

*Lederbett mit passendem Headboard, gerahmt*
*von „Trunk"-Kommoden. Jedes Domizil im*
*Wohnpalais verfügt über drei Schlafzimmer*

*Leather bed with matching headboard,*
*framed by "Trunk" chests of drawers. Each*
*Eisenzahn 1 home has three bedrooms*

15

Großzügige Küchen mit Flügeltüren in
die Halle sowie in den Essbereich sind
Markenzeichen der SCHMITZ-Grundrisse

Spacious kitchens with French doors
to the hall and dining area are a trademark
of RALF SCHMITZ floor plans

Ganz neue Maßstäbe in noblem Wohnen setzt das einzigartige Wohnpalais beim Kurfürstendamm. Berlins Prachtboulevard entstand auf Betreiben von Reichskanzler Bismarck persönlich als Pendant zu den Champs-Élysées von Paris – und so war es nur folgerichtig, dass Eisenzahn 1, der Inbegriff großbürgerlicher Wohnkultur, inspiriert ist von den exquisiten *appartements* und *avenues* der französischen Metropole. Die Fassade nimmt mit Gesimsen und tiefgezogenen Fenstern aber auch Elemente der für Charlottenburg-Wilmersdorf typischen Jahrhundertwendearchitektur auf.

Im Herzen des urban-gediegenen Westens der Hauptstadt entstand ein Meisterwerk, das herausragende Handwerkskunst und technische Ingenieurleistungen mit Stilsicherheit vereint: Der Architekt Sebastian Treese entwarf das symmetrische Gebäude, dessen Mitte ein Dachaufbau, das maßgeschmiedete Eingangsportal und ein sanft geschwungener Erker betonen, der sich zu beiden Seiten wiederholt. Plastizität gewinnt die Fassade auch durch ihre überdurchschnittliche Tiefe: über 50 Zentimeter, aufgebaut aus Stahlbeton, Dämmschicht und Ziegeln davor, die weiß verputzt sind. Alle Stuckprofile wurden ganz traditionell vor Ort von Hand gezogen. Schwarze Brüstungen aus Gusseisen bilden feine Ornamente; der Vorgarten sorgt für Abschirmung zur Eisenzahnstraße – der Gartenhof samt Loggia und Springbrunnen, zu dem sich ausladende Balkone öffnen, ist eine intime grüne Oase inmitten der Metropole.

Zwölf elegante Wohneinheiten beherbergt dieser edle Bau, darunter das luxuriöse Penthouse im gesamten Staffelgeschoss, das von einer Panorama-Dachterrasse gekrönt wird. Deckenhöhen zwischen 3,20 und 4,40 Metern und harmonisch ineinanderfließende Raumfolgen mit klassischen Proportionen kennzeichnen die Grundrisse.

Bottega Veneta, das berühmte italienische Luxus-Label, schuf in einer exklusiven Kooperation mit RALF SCHMITZ das Interieur der großzügigen Lobby und richtete eine elegante Musterwohnung ein: Kreativdirektor Tomas Maier wählte Möbel, Textilien und Accessoires aus der Bottega Veneta Home Collection aus, entschied über Wandfarben, Bodenbeläge und die Oberflächen der Einbauten.

Nun empfängt in der imposanten, 63 Quadratmeter großen Eingangshalle das legendärste Stück der Bottega Veneta Home Collection: der Bibliothekstisch, aus Holz mit Lederdetails maßgearbeitet. Die ikonischen Ledersofas „Meta" laden zum Verweilen ein. Alle Wandleuchten bestechen durch Details aus Intrecciato-Leder und ihr nobles Finish. Reliefs und Büsten suchte Tomas Maier in Berlins berühmter Gipsformerei aus – eine weitere Reverenz an die vollendete Eleganz eines klassischen Stilkanons, der diesen Neubau adelt.

---

RALF SCHMITZ's unique Eisenzahn 1 development in Berlin sets new standards in luxury living. It is situated on Eisenzahnstrasse, just off Kurfürstendamm, a magnificent tree-lined avenue created in 1875 at the behest of chancellor Otto von Bismarck as a counterpart to the Champs-Élysées. It is, then, entirely fitting that this superlative property should draw on the exquisite apartments of Parisian boulevards for inspiration. With its cornices and deep windows, however, the elegant façade also nods to the turn-of-the-century buildings that define this area's established architecture.

Situated in the refined heart of west Berlin, it is a veritable masterpiece, combining consummate style with outstanding craftsmanship and engineering. The design by architect Sebastian Treese features a symmetrical frontage whose centre is emphasised by the roof storey's projecting middle section, a bespoke hand-forged main entrance and a gently curving central oriel echoed by matching bays on either side. All the external plaster mouldings were traditionally crafted on site. Black cast-iron railings adorn the windows and fence the front garden off from the street, while the private rear courtyard garden, an urban oasis with loggia and fountain, is overlooked by generous balconies.

Inside, the twelve refined apartments, among them a fabulous full-floor penthouse topped by a roof terrace, offer flowing layouts with classically proportioned rooms. In an exclusive collaboration, one of these residences was turned into a show home with decors by Bottega Veneta. The luxury label's creative director Tomas Maier chose the furniture, textiles and accessories from its Home Collection and selected wall colours, flooring and the cabinetry's finishes. In the impressive 63-square-metre lobby, likewise decorated by BV, the Home Collection's legendary wooden Library Table, a meticulously crafted leather-inset piece, combines with inviting "Meta" sofas. There are also wall lights with eye-catching intrecciato leather details, plus reliefs and busts hand-picked by Maier at the famous Replica Workshop of the Prussian Cultural Heritage Foundation – a further reference to the classically inspired style of this spectacular building.

Im Esszimmer dominiert der runde
„Column"-Tisch mit schwarz-goldener
Marmorplatte, um ihn herum sind
Versionen des „Meta"-Stuhls versammelt.
„Drum"-Deckenleuchte aus Flechtleder

Paired with variants of the "Meta" chair,
a round "Column" table topped with
black-and-gold marble dominates the
dining room. Above is a "Drum"
pendant light with woven leather shade

*Privatlift in einer weiteren Wohnung,
einer weitläufigen Maisonette
mit insgesamt rund 260 qm Fläche*

*The private lift inside another of
the apartments, a spacious
maisonette of around 260 sqm*

20

*Glamourös belichtete, holzbelegte
Verbindungstreppe in der Maisonette*

*The maisonette's glamorously illuminated
internal wooden staircase*

*Zugang zur Musterwohnung vom
gemeinschaftlichen Treppenhaus mit Lift
rechts – als Blickfang dient dank des
raffinierten Grundrisses der Kamin*

*View into the show home from the main
staircase, with lift on the right. Well-
planned sight lines mean the eye is instantly
drawn to the elegant fireplace*

*Wandbündiger, verspiegelter Einbauschrank*
*mit Stauraum im Masterbad des Penthouse*

*A recessed mirrored cabinet adds storage space*
*to the penthouse's master bathroom*

*Zwei Waschtische aus erlesenem*
*Dietfurter Kalkstein mit schwungvollen*
*„Tara"-Armaturen von Dornbracht*

*Two washstands of exquisite*
*Dietfurt limestone with elegantly curved*
*"Tara" taps by Dornbracht*

*„Ein Penthouse ist eine feste Größe in einem*
*sich stetig verändernden Immobilienmarkt"*

*"A penthouse is a constant in*
*an ever-changing property market"*

*Die frei stehende Wanne „Celine" von Devon&Devon strahlt besonders vor der Schmuckwand aus Pietra Grigia*

*A feature wall of Pietra Grigia sets off the free-standing "Celine" bath by Devon&Devon*

Die 35 qm große Loggia zum intimen
Hofgarten unter einer Gewölbedecke

*The vaulted, 35-sqm loggia between foyer
and private courtyard garden*

*Die Rückfassade mit üppigen Balkonen zeigt ebenfalls von Hand gezogenen Stuck. Das Rasengrün ist sanft gestuft*

---

*Featuring large balconies, the rear façade has yet more handcrafted plaster mouldings. The lawn is subtly stepped*

*Eine Treillage portique, das klassische Rank- und Schmuckelement französischer Privatparks, bildet hinter dem Springbrunnen den Gartenabschluss*

---

*A portique de treillage, an ornamental trellis found in French formal gardens, adorns the perimeter beyond the fountain*

# AT A GLANCE: FOYERS & HALLS

ERLESENE LEUCHTEN SETZEN BÖDEN AUS NATURSTEIN IN SZENE.
SPIEGEL, KUNSTWERKE UND KONSOLEN ERGÄNZEN
DIE ENTREES – SO WIRD DAS ANKOMMEN AUSSERGEWÖHNLICH

LUXURIOUS LIGHTING AND FINE STONE FLOORING SET THE TONE,
MIRRORS, ARTWORKS AND CONSOLE TABLES PROVIDE
ELEGANT ACCENTS – RARELY HAS COMING HOME FELT SO SPECIAL

DÜSSELDORF, HAUS BERENGAR

*Kultiviert: Beidseitig riesige Spiegel,
Holztäfelungen, Stuck und eine
extrahohe Naturstein-Sockelleiste (2011)*

*Huge mirrors on each side, stucco, wood
panelling and high stone skirting
boards form an elegant ensemble (2011)*

DÜSSELDORF, MERCATORTERRASSEN

*Kontrastreich: Den markanten Marmorboden
in Schwarz-Weiß ergänzen zwei Säulen,
zarte Stuckleisten und Täfelungen (2011)*

*A black-and-white marble floor combines
strikingly with twin columns,
panelling and fine plasterwork (2011)*

DÜSSELDORF, PARKTERRASSEN

*Ein ausgeklügelter Leuchtkörpermix und der
Pietra-Grigia-Wandbrunnen prägen die von
Oliver Jungel gestaltete Halle (2014)*

*Oliver Jungel's foyer interior features
a sophisticated lighting mix and a
wall fountain in Pietra Grigia (2014)*

KEMPEN, KLOSTERHOF

*Reduziert: Subtile Raster setzen die
Akzente aus poliertem Bianco Carrara
in diesem Großprojekt (2014)*

*Polished Bianco Carrara accents
create a clean-lined grid effect at this
large-scale development (2014)*

DÜSSELDORF, HAUS HARDENBERG

*Glanzvoll: Stahl, Glas und eingelassene Wandspiegel weiten das Foyer mit Natursteinboden im Zooviertel (2008)*

*Steel, glass and inset mirrors bring an expansive feel to a shimmering stone-floored hall in Zooviertel (2008)*

DÜSSELDORF, HAUS ESPLANADE

*Rückbesinnung: In der Cecilienallee setzte RKW Architektur + gekonnt klassische Elemente wie Säulen ein (2015)*

*Classical details such as columns are cleverly integrated into our RKW-designed building on Cecilienallee (2015)*

BERLIN, HUBERTUSGÄRTEN

*Elegant: Ein fast deckenhoher Spiegel adelt einen der beiden Eingänge des Grunewalder Stadtvillen-Duos (2010)*

*An almost ceiling-high mirror graces one of the handsome hallways at these twin Grunewald villas (2010)*

DÜSSELDORF, SOPHIENHOF

*Gediegen: klare grafische Raster bei Tür, Bodenbelag und Wandgestaltung in monochromem Chic (2008)*

*The clean, grid-like lines of floor, door and walls give further definition to a chic monochrome foyer (2008)*

BERLIN, WISSMANNSTRASSE

*Kunstvoll: Grazile Konsolen aus Metall und Schiefer, handgefertigt im Atelier Stefan Leo, stehen im Grunewald-Domizil (2016)*

*Slender metal-and-slate console tables, handcrafted by Atelier Stefan Leo, adorn this Grunewald hall (2016)*

# REPORT: HISTORY

Tradition verpflichtet: Seit 1864 ist der Name
Schmitz ein Synonym für Baukunst,
nun in *fünfter Generation*. Eine Firmenbiografie

Dedicated to Tradition: The Schmitz family
name has been synonymous with the
art of construction *since 1864*. A brief history

TEXT BETTINA SCHNEUER    FOTOS GREGOR HOHENBERG, ANDREAS GEHRKE, RALF SCHMITZ, BILDARCHIV DER STADT KEMPEN

*Peter Heinrich Schmitz (1831–1908) gründete in Grefrath eine Schreinerei,
wenige Jahre später kam eine kleine Baufirma hinzu ——— Peter Heinrich Schmitz
(1831–1908) founded a joinery in Grefrath and later a building firm*

S ie ist das Gegenteil von Trends: die Tradition. Ohne
ihre Wurzeln gibt es kein Wachstum – und keine Schönheit,
denn Schönheit speist sich immer auch aus Erfahrung, also aus
Geschichte.

Architektur ist gebaute Geschichte. Meist jedoch wird
sie unter dem Blickwinkel der Entwerfenden betrachtet, nur
selten aus anderen Perspektiven beleuchtet. Dabei ist gerade
ein Projektentwickler, also der Auftraggeber, im Bauprozess
„der Dirigent, der Partitur, Orchester und Publikum gleicher-
maßen im Blick haben muss", wie es der bekannte Berliner
Architekt Paul Kahlfeldt formuliert: „Und die Unternehmerfamilie Schmitz versteht sich als Dirigent, sie baut eben so, als
baue sie für sich selbst – nur eben im Vielen."

Die Baubiografie beginnt 1864, als Peter Heinrich Schmitz
in Grefrath am Niederrhein eine Baufirma gründet und die
Tradition der Familie als Handwerksleute etabliert. Nach dem
Bau von Kirchen, Klöstern und Fabriken in der Umgebung
entsteht 1896 die erste Villa im Auftrag eines Textilfabri-
kanten – sie markiert den Beginn des Bauens auch im hochwertigen Wohnsegment. Der drittgeborene Sohn, Heinrich
Schmitz, gründet knapp zehn Jahre später die Niederlassung in
Kempen, die er ab 1919 allein als Heinrich Schmitz KG führt.

*Spezialisierung im Sakralbau: Das eindrucksvolle Kloster Arca Pacis (heute Abtei Mariendonk) entstand von 1899 bis 1901 bei Grefrath* —— *Focus on ecclesiastical architecture: the impressive monastery near Grefrath, today the Mariendonk Abbey, was completed in 1901*

Er errichtet in Kempen unter anderem Villen, Wohnhäuser und das Königliche Lehrerseminar, das 1925 zum Gymnasium Thomaeum wird; hier sind bislang drei Generationen der Familie zur Schule gegangen!

1945 tritt Hieronymus Schmitz, jüngster Sohn von Heinrich Schmitz, in die Firma ein, die nun in dritter Generation familiengeführt wird. Der Architekt, der bei Heinrich Tessenow studiert hatte, geht mit Elan und Kompetenz daran, den kriegsgebeutelten Betrieb neu aufzustellen und an die tradierte Bauqualität anzuknüpfen; er entwirft auch selbst, etwa 1952/53 die Blockrandbebauung in Kempen am Bahnhof. Man engagiert sich im Wohnungshoch- und Siedlungsbau und entwickelt dies zum Kerngeschäft der Wiederaufbaujahre. Geografisch werden ganz neue Regionen wie Düsseldorf, Essen und Köln erschlossen. Mit einem Beitrag über ein Landhaus am Niederrhein würdigt 1961 die Architekturzeitschrift *Baumeister* die Leistungen des Unternehmens bei der Errichtung gediegener Villen. 1971 entsteht in Düsseldorf ein ambitioniertes Hochhaus am Hofgarten mit 13 Wohn- und sechs Büroetagen; im angeschlossenen zweigeschossigen Pavillon bezieht die in der Enkelgeneration zum Großunternehmen aufgestiegene Firma neue Räume. Mehrere hundert Mitarbeiter bieten nun ein Spektrum an Leistungen vom Roh- bis zum Innenausbau. Ganze Stadtteile werden aus dem Nichts erbaut.

## IN DER ENKELGENERATION WÄCHST DIE BAUFIRMA UND WIRD ZUR WOHNUNGSBAUGESELLSCHAFT.

Als jedoch der Markt in den 70er-Jahren zunehmend gesättigt ist, konzentriert sich Ralf Schmitz – also die nunmehr vierte Generation – auf die Errichtung besonders hochwertiger Wohnanlagen und gründet 1977 mit gerade 24 Jahren seine eigene Wohnungsbaugesellschaft in Kempen.

In kurzer Zeit etabliert er das Unternehmen mit dem Bau hochwertiger Eigentumswohnungen in Kempen, Krefeld und Düsseldorf. Eine Anlage für betreutes Wohnen im Alter macht die Firma 1992 zum Pionier auch auf diesem Gebiet. Parallel zur Neubautätigkeit werden Bestandsbauten und insbesondere Baudenkmäler saniert und modernisiert – 1998 die Villa Brandenburg in Kempen, die bis heute der Stammsitz des Unternehmens ist. Den Schritt nach Berlin wagt die Firma 2004. Zwei stilvolle Stadthäuser im noblen Grunewald setzen ein erstes Zeichen. Parallel werden in Düsseldorf diverse neue markante Objekte geplant und realisiert. Immer komplexer wird jedoch das Ausfindigmachen bebaubarer Grundstücke in guten bis sehr guten Wohnlagen dieser Großstädte. 2007 wird die Hauptstadt-Niederlassung weiter ausgebaut und zum Synonym für die Entwicklung hochwertiger Immobilien, auch dank der intensiven Zusammenarbeit mit verschiedenen renommierten Architekten wie schon in Düsseldorf.

Baustart des Klosterhofs, des bis dato größten Projekts, ist 2011 in Kempen. Wenig später entsteht aus der Schmitz-Wohnungsbaugesellschaft die Ralf Schmitz GmbH & Co. KGaA; bis heute ist der inhabergeführte Betrieb zu 100 Prozent im Besitz der Familie. 2013 wird auch das erste Immobilienprojekt der Niederlassung Hamburg im feinen Othmarschen vollendet – das Berliner Architektenpaar Petra und Paul Kahlfeldt zeichnet für den Entwurf verantwortlich.

Zum 150-jährigen Jubiläum des Traditionsunternehmens 2014 wird der neue Düsseldorfer Sitz am Rheinufer in Oberkassel bezogen. Zudem erscheint die aufwendige Monografie *Architektur und Handwerk* im Jovis Verlag, eine facettenreiche Dokumentation der klassisch-eleganten Bauten der Unternehmerfamilie Schmitz.

Ende 2016 wird weltweit über die Fertigstellung des prestigeträchtigen Wohnpalais Eisenzahn 1 beim Kurfürstendamm berichtet, für das erstmalig und exklusiv die italienische Luxusmarke Bottega Veneta mit einem deutschen Bauunternehmen kooperiert. Aktuell sind diverse neue repräsentative Vorhaben an allen Standorten im Bau oder unter Planung. Und so zeigt sich, dass noch immer und seit über 150 Jahren das Leitmotiv des Firmengründers Peter Heinrich Schmitz gültig bleibt: „Nur Wert hat Bestand."

*Erster Villenbau durch Firma Schmitz: Das ambitionierte Anwesen für Dietrich Girmes entstand 1896 in Grefrath-Oedt, zehn Jahre zuvor hatte man bereits eine große Textilfabrik für die Familie errichtet —— The Schmitz firm's first villa, an ambitious estate for Dietrich Girmes, was built in 1896*

*Das Kempener Lehrerseminar wurde
1925 zum Gymnasium* ───────
*The Royal Teaching College of Kempen
became a grammar school in 1925*

*Ab 1905 in Kempen: Heinrich Schmitz (1870–1952)*
─── *Since 1905 in Kempen: Heinrich Schmitz*

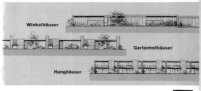

**NEUE STADT HOCHDAHL**

HEINRICH SCHMITZ

*Erkrath-Hochdahl: 320 Wohnungen
und 130 Einfamilienhäuser* ───────
*Erkrath-Hochdahl: 320 apartments
and 130 single-family homes*

*Prospekt zur 1974 fertiggestellten Großsiedlung*
─── *Catalogue for a residential development*

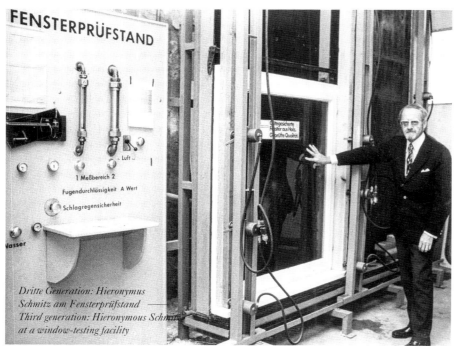

FENSTERPRÜFSTAND

*Dritte Generation: Hieronymus
Schmitz am Fensterprüfstand
Third generation: Hieronymous Schmitz
at a window-testing facility*

*Hochhaus der
Heinrich Schmitz
KG am Hofgarten,
Düsseldorf 1971*

*High-rise offices of
Heinrich Schmitz KG
in Düsseldorf 1971*

The antithesis of trend is tradition. Without tradition's deep roots there can be no growth – and no beauty, because beauty always draws from experience, and therefore history.

## IN THE THIRD GENERATION, THE CONSTRUCTION FIRM TURNED INTO A HOUSE-BUILDING DEVELOPER.

Architecture is a form of constructed history. However, it is usually regarded only from the creator's vantage point and rarely illuminated from other perspectives. But it is often the developer and client, the "director" of the building process, "who must have an overview equally of the score, orchestra and audience," as renowned architect Paul Kahlfeldt describes it. "And the Schmitz family firm understands itself as the director; they approach each project as if for themselves – just in multiples."

The firm's history began in 1864 when Peter Heinrich Schmitz founded a construction company in Grefrath am Niederrhein, establishing a family tradition of craftsmanship. After erecting churches, cloisters and factories in the region, the Schmitz company built their first villa in 1896 on commission from a textile manufacturer, marking the start of business in the premium residential segment. The third-born son, Heinrich Schmitz, founded the office in Kempen some ten years later, which he continued to lead as Heinrich Schmitz KG after 1919. In Kempen, Schmitz built villas, residential buildings and the Royal Teaching College, which became Gymnasium Thomaeum in 1925 and has schooled three generations of the family.

In 1945, Hieronymus Schmitz, Heinrich Schmitz's youngest son, joined the firm, by then in the hands of the third generation of the family. He approached his work with verve and knowhow, striving to renew operations after years of war and to draw on the family's long-time quality standards. During the years of German national reconstruction, apartment and residential developments became central to the firm's business, and new cities such as Düsseldorf, Essen and Cologne were added to the firm's portfolio. In 1961, the architecture magazine *Baumeister* honoured the firm's construction of refined villas with an article about a Schmitz-designed country house in the Lower Rhine region. In 1971, the Schmitz company moved into their new Düsseldorf offices in an ambitious tower at the Hofgarten that boasted six office and thirteen residential floors. By then, the company had grown to more than one hundred employees and offered a spectrum of services from initial construction to interior design.

P. H. Schmitz & C°

HEINRICH SCHMITZ KG

Schmitz KG

RALF SCHMITZ

RS

RALF SCHMITZ

*Zum 150-jährigen Jubiläum erschien eine Monografie. Die Logos zeigen die Unternehmensentwicklung seit 1864 —— A monograph celebrated the firm's 150th anniversary. The company's logo development since 1864*

As the market became increasingly saturated in the 1970s, however, Ralf Schmitz – the firm's fourth-generation son – concentrated on the development of particularly high-quality residential estates and founded his own company in Kempen in 1977 at the age of just 24. The firm established itself in no time with its refined freehold flats in Kempen, Krefeld and Düsseldorf.

The company made its first foray into Berlin in 2004; two refined city villas in the well-heeled district of Grunewald were markers of the things to come. Simultaneously a diverse group of new, striking sites were planned and realised in Düsseldorf. Finding suitable real estate in good and excellent residential areas in these urban hubs has become increasingly complex. The Berlin branch of the Schmitz company has since become synonymous with the development of high-quality real estate, thanks in part to its intensive collaboration with numerous renowned architects, as has been the practice in Düsseldorf.

The Schmitz-Wohnungsbaugesellschaft was reconstituted as Ralf Schmitz GmbH & Co. KGaA. The firm remains entirely family-run and is owned 100 per cent by the family. In 2013, the Hamburg office's first real estate project was completed in the upscale Othmarschen district. On the occasion of its 150th anniversary, the monograph *Architektur und Handwerk* was published by Jovis, providing a multifaceted documentation of the classical and elegant buildings built by the Schmitz family.

In late 2016, the international press cheered the completion of the prestigious Eisenzahn 1 near Berlin's Kurfürstendamm – the first and exclusive collaboration between Italian luxury brand Bottega Veneta and a German development group. Various new projects are currently under construction or in planning, thus proving that founder Peter Heinrich Schmitz's guiding mandate has withstood the test of 150 years' time: "Only value will endure."

*Vierte und fünfte Generation bilden zusammen die Geschäftsführung: Ralf Schmitz und seine Söhne Richard Alexander und Axel Martin (sitzend) am Standort Berlin* —— *The fourth and fifth generations manage the firm: Ralf Schmitz, his sons Richard Alexander and Axel Martin (seated) in Berlin*

# HAUS BAHREN, HAMBURG

NAHE DER BERÜHMTEN ELBCHAUSSEE ANKERT
DIESER NOBLE NEUBAU. EIN RUNDGANG
DURCH DIE *LUXURIÖSE SHOWROOM-WOHNUNG*

LOCATED CLOSE TO THE RIVER ELBE, THIS
ELEGANT, FREE-STANDING  BUILDING
IS HOME TO A *SUMPTUOUS SHOW APARTMENT*

FOTOS **GREGOR HOHENBERG, ANDREAS GEHRKE**    TEXT **BETTINA SCHNEUER**

*Kaminsalon im Hochparterre:*
*Die Clubsessel sind ebenso wie Deckenleuchte*
*und Beistelltische Unikatentwürfe*

*The show home's fireside club chairs*
*are bespoke originals, as are*
*the ceiling lamps and coffee tables*

Das Living bietet 42 qm Fläche; Parkett
aus kerngeräucherter Eiche ziert die
insgesamt drei Räume zum großen Garten

The living room measures 42 sqm; all
three rooms facing the large garden have core-
smoked oak parquet flooring

36

**P**assend zur gediegenen Zurückhaltung, die man im schönsten Viertel der Hansestadt, in Othmarschen, kultiviert, entstand der Solitär von RALF SCHMITZ. Der Gebäude-sockel aus Muschelkalk hebt den klaren Baukörper am Roosens Weg 5 mit seinen horizontalen Linien empor; vier Säulen markieren das Entree, ein Bezug auf das Jenisch Haus und dessen prächtigen Park gleich ums Eck ebenso wie auf die klassischen Elbvillen.

Eine der Hochparterre-Wohnungen wurde als *showflat* eingerichtet: Auf knapp 160 Quadratmetern, in fünf Zimmern und zwei Bädern, tummelt sich ein souveräner Stilkosmos, der Erprobtes versammelt und durch neue, wesensverwandte Eigenkreationen aus dem Hause RALF SCHMITZ ergänzt. Tragende Rollen spielen erstens die hochwertigen Materi-alien: edle natürliche Stoffe, Hölzer und Naturstein, dazu schimmernde Akzente aus Messing, hochglanzpoliert oder brüniert. Zweitens die Farben: lichtes Zink, warmes Creme und kreidiges Weiß, eine Palette, wie sie schon im georgia-nischen England in Adelshäusern beliebt war. Drittens der Grundriss: Drei Salons, verbunden durch Flügeltüren, bilden eine Enfilade zum Garten und zur Terrasse.

Schon im Foyer zeigt sich, viertens, was ein Interieur à la RALF SCHMITZ auszeichnet. Die rasante Hell-Dunkel-Geometrie des Bodens aus portugiesischem Marmor-Kalkstein beleuchten zwei Ikosaeder, die einem Entwurf von Josef Hoffmann nachempfunden sind.

Auf dem Parkett aus kerngeräucherter Eiche im zentralen Wohnraum, mit 42 Quadratmetern gründerzeitlich üppig bemessen, steht ein SCHMITZ-Sofa, gefertigt in den berühmten Ateliers Charles Jouffre – sie arbeiten auch für Hermès, Chanel und Luxushotels –, bei einem Tisch mit Holzplatte und kaltgezogenem Stahlgestell, der eigens in der Berliner Manufaktur Stefan Leo entstand. Durchdacht und mondän ist die Küche mit raffiniert schimmernden Fronten aus brüniertem Messing mit Textil-Glas-Einsätzen: Hier können, auch dank des Herds von La Cornue, herrliche Menüs entstehen und dann am nierenförmigen Tisch der auf Maß gefertigten Sitzecke verspeist werden. Das Kamin-zimmer schmücken Ledersessel, die wirken, als stammten sie aus einem britischen Club, jedoch Neuentwürfe sind. Im Schlafzimmer dominiert das Bettunikat mit Headboard, ein von Jouffre umgesetzter SCHMITZ-Entwurf.

Das Masterbad aus rauchgrauem Naturstein, dezent geädert, erinnert an Landsitz-Ästhetik, ebenso die Wanne vor dem Fenster – alle technischen Details dagegen, die Objekte und Armaturen von Bette, Dornbracht und Villeroy & Boch, sind *state of the art* der Neuzeit. Hochmodern sind auch jene Elemente, die Komfort und Sicherheit bedeuten: elektrisch betriebene Aluminiumrollläden mit Hochschiebeschutz, raumweise steuerbar auch via Smartphone, ebenso wie das P4A-Glas mit sogenannten Alarmspinnen, das die klassischen Sprossenfenster und Fenstertüren schützt.

---

Situated in Othmarschen, Hamburg's finest neighbourhood, this new-build is entirely in keeping with the exclusive surroundings. Its façade features clean lines above a band of fossiliferous limestone, while the quartet of columns flanking the entrance is a nod to the nearby Jenisch Haus.

One of the apartments has been decorated as a show home. A property with two bathrooms and a floor area of almost 160 square metres, it offers sumptuously stylish interiors that blend classic designs with bespoke pieces by the firm's in-house designers. High-quality materials are an integral part of this harmonious mix, with velvet, natural stone, oak and marble to the fore and burnished or gloss-finish brass accents playing an eye-catching supporting role. The colour schemes are dominated by pale zinc, warm cream and chalky white while the layout boasts an enfilade of three spacious salons, connected by double doors, that is accessed via an elegant foyer and opens onto the terrace and garden. The distinctive SCHMITZ signature is apparent as soon as you enter the

hall, where light-and-dark floor tiles of Portuguese marbled limestone are arranged in a striking geometric pattern. The 42-square-metre living room's exclusive furnishings include a SCHMITZ sofa made by the famous Ateliers Charles Jouffre, a firm whose clients include Hermès and luxury hotels. The kitchen is elegantly refined, with unit fronts featuring glass-and-fabric panels framed in gleaming burnished brass and equipped with a high-end La Cornue range. Another living room has inviting new fireside leather armchairs that could be straight out of an English gentlemen's club. The bedroom is dominated by a bespoke bed with headboard, while the subtly veined stone throughout gives the master bathroom a country house feel. Functionally, though, it is resolutely contemporary, thanks to a flush-fitted shower with fixtures and fittings by Bette, Dornbracht and Villeroy+Boch.

Other features include roller blinds controllable via smart-phone and break-in-resistant glass with alarm loops that protect the traditional multi-pane windows and French doors.

Ein SCHMITZ-Sofa, gefertigt in den
berühmten Ateliers Charles Jouffre,
plus das neu bezogene Vintage-Sesselduo
rahmen den Tisch mit kaltgezogenem
Stahlgestell, der eigens in der Berliner
Manufaktur Stefan Leo entstand

Supported by a cold-drawn steel frame,
the bespoke table by Berlin's Atelier
Stefan Leo anchors a pair of
reupholstered vintage armchairs and
a SCHMITZ sofa made at the famous
Ateliers Charles Jouffre, Paris

Die helle Ankleide ist ein deckenhohes
Stauraumwunder mit raffiniertem
Schuhauszug und charmanter Sitznische

A marvel of floor-to-ceiling storage,
the airy dressing room features a pull-out
shoe rack and an inviting window seat

Über Nachttischen aus Eiche
mit x-förmiger Beinlösung funkeln
die Aalto-Klassiker „A330S"

Alvar Aalto's classic "A330S" lamps hang
above oak side tables with x-shaped legs

„Edle natürliche Stoffe, Hölzer und Naturstein,
dazu schimmernde Akzente aus Messing"

"First-class natural stone, fabrics and wood,
combined with accents of gleaming brass"

*Im Schlafraum dominiert das Bettunikat mit Headboard, ein von Jouffre mit Designers-Guild-Stoff umgesetzter SCHMITZ-Entwurf*

*The bespoke bed boasts a SCHMITZ headboard produced by Jouffre and upholstered in a Designers Guild fabric*

*Durchdachte Menü-Werkstatt: ein mondäner Herd von La Cornue plus eine maßgefertigte Sitzecke mit Nierentisch, dazu passen die kugeligen Scarpa-Leuchten aus den Sixties*

*A stylish setting for culinary creations: featuring a high-end La Cornue range and a bespoke breakfast area with a kidney-shaped table and rounded 1960s Scarpa pendants*

*Der geäderte Naturstein erinnert an Landgut-Ästhetik, ebenso die Wanne vor dem Fenster – dagegen sind die Objekte und Armaturen von Villeroy & Boch, Bette und Dornbracht Klassiker der Neuzeit*

*Like the bathtub by the window, the veined natural stone channels a country house style; the fixtures and fittings by Dornbracht, Bette and Villeroy & Boch are modern classics*

# AT A GLANCE: LIFTS

RAUF ODER RUNTER – NUR ZWEI OPTIONEN BIETET DER AUFZUG.
GESTALTERISCH JEDOCH SIND FABELHAFT VIELFÄLTIGE
LÖSUNGEN DENKBAR. EINE STILSCHAU VERTIKALER MOBILITÄT

---

UP OR DOWN? THEY MAY ONLY GO IN TWO
DIRECTIONS BUT, DESIGN-WISE, LIFTS OFFER A WHOLE HOST OF
POSSIBILITIES, AS THIS ELEVATING SELECTION SHOWS

**DÜSSELDORF, MERCATORTERRASSEN**

*Gestaltet in Schwarz-Weiß, wird die
strenge Symmetrie von Vestibül und Lift dank
Stuck und Säulen heiterer (2011)*

*Plasterwork and pillars brighten the
strictly symmetrical black-and-white
look of vestibule and lift (2011)*

**BERLIN, HAUS LUDWIG**

*Eine beeindruckende Supraporte aus
Naturstein krönt den Zugang zum Aufzug,
den eine Lichtdecke erhellt (2013)*

*An impressive stone lintel tops the
entrance to this lift, which is exquisitely
lit by an illuminated ceiling (2008)*

**KEMPEN, PETERSTRASSE**

*Helle und Komfort: Der verspiegelte Lift bringt
Flair in das Ensemble aus Baudenkmal
und Luxusneubau im klassischen Stil (2017)*

*Light and luxury: mirror walls enhance
this ensemble of historic original
and classically styled new-build (2017)*

**DÜSSELDORF, BANKSTRASSE**

*Dunkle Opulenz für Haus Battenberg
in Golzheim mit vornehm
betonter Deckenleuchte (2013)*

*Dark opulence plus an eye-catchingly
elegant ceiling light greet residents
at Golzheim's Haus Battenberg (2013)*

# CRAFT & TRADITION

STUCK, SCHMIEDEKUNST UND TREPPEN: *EXKLUSIVE BAUELEMENTE*, ALLE GEFERTIGT VON *MEISTERN IHRES FACHES*

MOULDINGS, METALWORK AND STAIRS: *FINE ARCHITECTURAL FEATURES* MADE BY *MASTERS OF THEIR TRADE*

*Mit eigens gefertigten Schablonen wird per Hand und direkt auf der Baustelle des Berliner Wohnpalais Eisenzahn 1 aus einer zementbasierten Masse der Stuck gezogen*

*Work-in-progress at Eisenzahn 1: cement-based plaster ornaments handcrafted on site with the aid of bespoke running moulds*

*Schmuckelemente geben Fassaden
Plastizität und Eleganz – seit der Antike
eine wichtige Gestaltungstechnik, die
Gebäuden zeitlose Schönheit verleiht*

*Adding sculptural details and elegance
to a façade, plaster mouldings
have been used to refine the appearance
of buildings since ancient times*

*„Weit auskragende Profile, sehr
präzise vom Architekten geplant"*

*"Prominent plaster mouldings made to the
architect's very precise specifications"*

*Ornament ist Versprechen: Schwungvolle
Gesimse betonen die drei Erker von
Eisenzahn 1 und verleihen der groß-
bürgerlichen Straßenfront Leichtigkeit*

*Curving cornices emphasise the three oriels of
Eisenzahn 1, giving its grand frontage a
lightness reminiscent of Art Nouveau façades*

Mittelalter und Moderne: Hammer, Amboss
und Zangen, glimmender Schmiedekoks – alles
dient in der Berliner Metall- und Kunstschmiede
Fittkau (oben) noch heute zur Fertigung
filigraner Schmuckteile, etwa der Schnörkel
(links) für die Zaunanlage von Eisenzahn 1

*Medieval meets modern: at the Fittkau metal
workshops in Berlin, delicate ornaments
such as this flourish for the Eisenzahn 1 fence
(left) are still made using the time-honoured
tools of forge hammer, anvil and tongs*

Welche Zartheit sich starren Werkstoffen
entlocken lässt, zeigt etwa die Maske eines
Jünglings, von Hand getrieben aus Zinn

*A handcrafted tin mask of a boy's
head illustrates the delicate forms that can
be wrought from hard metals*

„Wir setzen auf Hand und Werk,
auf Menschen, auf ihr Können und
auf gewachsene Techniken"

"We put our faith in people and their skills
and in well-developed techniques"

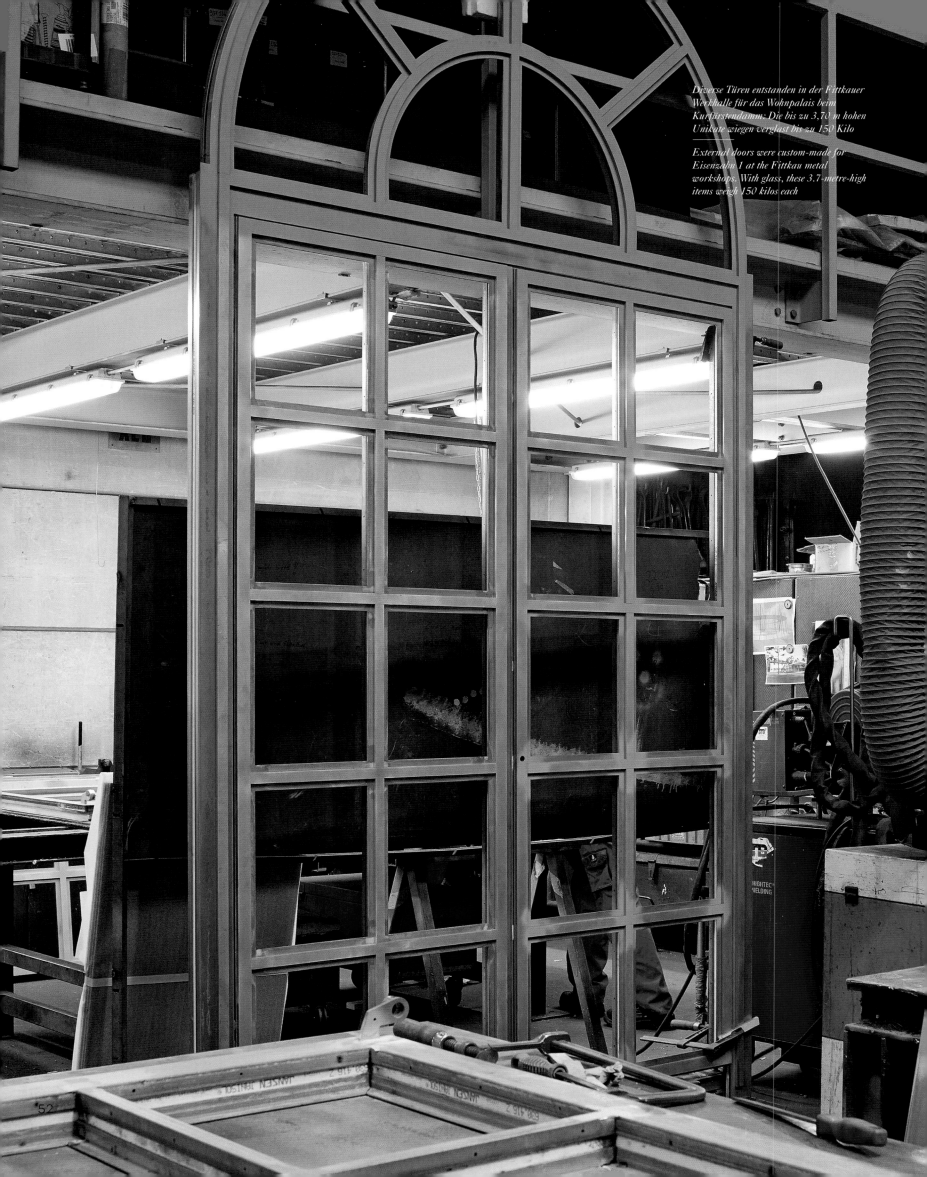

Diverse Türen entstanden in der Fittkauer
Werkhalle für das Wohnpalais beim
Kurfürstendamm: Die bis zu 3,70 m hohen
Unikate wiegen verglast bis zu 150 Kilo

External doors were custom-made for
Eisenzahn 1 at the Fittkau metal
workshops. With glass, these 3.7-metre-high
items weigh 150 kilos each

S tuck ist der Glanz alter Zeiten und traditionelles Kunsthandwerk, kein Luxus", sagt Ulrich Jacobi. Seit über einem Vierteljahrhundert arbeiten der Meister und seine fast 20 Mitarbeiter daran, historische Bauten wieder schön und neue Gebäude prächtiger zu machen. Für das Berliner Wohnpalais Eisenzahn 1 lieferte Jacobis Team über tausend Meter handgefertigte Stuckleisten für die Wohnungen; die dafür eigens gebauten Schablonen aus Holz und Blech umfassten 15 verschiedene Motive. Das optisch so leicht wirkende Gipsornament ist schwer: Jedes Profil wiegt bis zu acht Kilo. Rund 400 Stück entstanden in der Werkstatt in Alt-Hohenschönhausen: Gießen, Armieren mit Jute, Gießen, Ziehen – Gießen, Armieren ... Mindestens zwanzigmal wird dieser Vorgang wiederholt, bis ein perfektes Profil entstanden ist. Schnell muss es dabei zugehen, denn die flüssige Mischung ist temperamentvoll: „Ihre Konsistenz kann sich von Minute zu Minute ändern. Je länger Gips gebrannt wurde, desto länger kann er Flüssigkeit aufnehmen und ist damit besser zu verarbeiten", erklärt Jacobi.

„Weit auskragende Profile aus massivem zementbasiertem Mörtel, sehr präzise vom Architekten geplant", befindet Klaus-Dieter Müller über die Front von Eisenzahn 1. „Großartig auch, dass die Fassade zum Hof ebenso schmuckvoll ist wie die zur Straße." Müller ist Stuckateurmeister, Restaurator im Stuckateurhandwerk, Obermeister der Baugewerks-Innung Berlin – und geschäftsführender Gesellschafter der K. Rogge Spezialbau GmbH. In über 50 Jahren ist das Unternehmen auf rund 200 Mitarbeiter gewachsen und stolz auf Sanierungen wie die des Reichstags, des Pergamonmuseums sowie auf zahllose Arbeiten bei bundesweiten Neubauten von Hotels bis zu Flughäfen. „Keine Maschine, die in China steht, keine Fertigprofile aus Styropor mit Überzug: Wir setzen auf Hand und Werk, auf Menschen, auf ihr Können und auf gewachsene Techniken", sagt Müller. Die Fassaden von Eisenzahn 1 sind angelehnt an Schinkels preußisch-aufgeklärte Klassik, umso präziser musste der reduzierte Vertikalstuck gearbeitet werden. „Der gesamte Außenputz, alle Profilierungen wurden vor Ort mittels selbst gebauter Schablone gezogen." Die Arbeit für ein Unternehmen wie RALF SCHMITZ mit ausgesprochen hohen Qualitätsansprüchen sei daher „ein Traum", denn man räume „der Handwerkskunst sehr hohen Stellenwert ein".

Eine Hommage an das Handwerk und ein Spannungsbogen vom Alten zur Suche nach neuen Ausdrucksformen sind auch die Treppenunikate von Pergande. Die Berliner Zimmermeister arbeiten seit über 75 Jahren und in der dritten Familiengeneration. In der Spandauer Werkstatt sowie direkt auf der Baustelle entsteht statt Massenware nachhaltige Ästhetik für Schritt und Tritt, die man schon lange auch bei RALF SCHMITZ schätzt.

Holz lässt sich in viele Formen bringen, es passt sich seiner Umgebung an. Das bedeutet aber nicht, dass es in seiner Umgebung untergeht. Neben der kunstfertigen Leistung des Zimmermanns wird der Raumeindruck einer Treppe durch die Qualität des Holzes bestimmt. Jeder Stamm, der verarbeitet wird, fällt in Farbe und Struktur anders aus. Auch Farbunterschiede zwischen Langholz und Hirnholz beweisen die Unverwechselbarkeit des Materials – bei Pergande verarbeitet man daher nur Ausgewähltes aus bestimmten Wäldern, damit die fertige Treppe als funktionale Komponente ebenso wie als gestalterisch-repräsentativer Eyecatcher eines Gebäudes Wirkung entfaltet.

Kraft und Feingefühl erfordert auch jenes uralte Handwerk, dem die Griechen einst einen eigenen Gott zuordneten. Es schafft aus starren Stoffen Schönes – und dabei geht es laut zu: Krachend donnert der vier Kilo schwere Schmiedehammer auf das glühende Eisen, das durch Hitze weich wurde und sich nun formen lässt, als sei es Knete. Doch Wucht alleine reicht nicht. Präzision, Technik und Augenmaß müssen dazukommen, um Eisen, Stahl oder Bronze in elegante Fenstergitter zu verwandeln, in Geländer, Zäune, Tore. Schmuck für Schlösser ebenso wie für Häuser, hart im Nehmen und zart bis prunkvoll in den Formen. Vielleicht hatte Goethe speziell an die Schmiede gedacht, als er befand: „Aller Kunst muss das Handwerk vorausgehen."

Stefan Fittkaus Firma – 2002 übernahm er die 1926 gegründete Kunstschmiede – ist auf aufwendige Metallarbeiten spezialisiert. In der Werkhalle in Berlin-Weißensee entstanden etwa Türgriffe für das Luxushotel „Adlon", das Tor zum Barockschloss-Gästehaus der Bundesregierung, und ebenso das Tor des Bodemuseums.

Für das Wohnpalais Eisenzahn 1 fertigte man die 3,70 Meter emporragende Hauseingangstür und deren kleinere Geschwister zum Hof. Zwei Wochen dauerte es, bis die imposanten Unikate fertig waren für die Lackierung in Schwarz. Mit Glaseinsätzen wiegt eine Tür 150 Kilo. „Das voluminöse Vordach, ein in Paris um 1900 typisches Bauteil, war eine technische Herausforderung – wir haben eine 3-D-Statik angewandt. Es gelten heute ja viel mehr Auflagen als vor über 100 Jahren", sagt Stefan Fittkau. Doch die Werkzeuge bleiben traditionell: Hammer, Amboss, Zangen, der glimmende Schmiedekoks, die Balancé zum Pressen und

Prägen. „Sieht immer ein bisschen aus wie im Mittelalter", sagt ein altgedienter Mitarbeiter über das Ambiente.

Über 100 Zierelemente für den Zaun des Wohnpalais entstanden von Hand: Schnörkel, die an Äste oder Blattumrisse erinnern. Hier musste deren Gestalter den Überblick behalten, denn Abweichungen werden nur im Millimeterbereich geduldet – vor Ort zusammengefügt soll sich ja ein perfektes Bild ergeben. Der Einbau der Türen war dann ein großer Moment, einer, der wieder jene Kraft und jenes Feingefühl erfordert, die schon ihre Entstehung prägten. Und auch ein großer Moment für jedes Haus als Markierung seiner Schwelle: Hier beginnt – Zuhause.

---

"Plasterwork is about old-time opulence and traditional craftsmanship, it's not about luxury," says Ulrich Jacobi. For over a quarter of a century, this master plasterer and his team have been restoring historic buildings to their former glory as well as refining new-builds with time-honoured techniques. For the prestigious Eisenzahn 1 development, they produced over a thousand metres of handcrafted plasterwork, using specially made wood-and-tin moulds to create the 15 different designs for the apartments. Around 400 separate mouldings weighing up to eight kilograms each were made; each had to be cast, wrapped in jute scrim, cast, run, then cast and wrapped again – a process repeated at least 20 times until the moulding is exactly right. During the production, speed is also of the essence because the liquid mix is capricious: "Its consistency can change from one minute to the next. The longer plaster has been fired, the longer it can absorb liquid and the easier it is to work with," explains Jacobi. The building's frontage has "prominent mouldings made of solid cement-based plaster to the architect's very precise specifications," observes Klaus-Dieter Müller, who is also impressed that "the rear is just as decorative as the street elevation." The master plasterer and restorer is director of the Building Trades Guild of Berlin and managing partner at K. Rogge Spezialbau GmbH. Employing around 200 people, this 50-year-old company has a proud history of restorations including the Reichstag building and Berlin's Pergamon Museum as well as a portfolio spanning everything from hotels to airports. "No Chinese-based production here, no off-the-shelf mouldings in coated polystyrene; we put our faith in hands and craft, in people and their skills and in well-developed techniques," Müller says. The façades at Eisenzahn 1 feature pared-down vertical mouldings that required particular precision of the plasterers. "We had to run all the external plasterwork on site using a custom-made mould." Working for a firm with such exceptionally high standards as RALF SCHMITZ, though, is "a dream" because "so much store is set by craftsmanship." This fusion of craft traditions and today's search for new expressive forms can also be seen in the work of Pergande, a Berlin-based family firm now in third-generation ownership. At their workshop in Spandau and on site, Pergande's master carpenters build bespoke staircases that offer the kind of enduring quality the name RALF SCHMITZ has long stood for.

Wood is easy to shape into different forms and thus adapt to particular settings. That's not to say it fades into the background however. In fact, the look and feel of a staircase is determined both by the technical skill of the carpenter and by the quality of the wood. No two trunks are identical in colour and structure, while even the end grain and long grain of a piece can exhibit different hues. Pergande uses only carefully chosen timber from selected forests, thus ensuring the finished functional staircase acts as an aesthetic eye-catcher as well.

The combination of brawn and dexterity is also the bedrock of another time-honoured trade. Brute force plus precision, technique and a fine eye are required to transform iron, steel, or bronze into refined railings, fences and gates. This complex decorative metalwork is Stefan Fittkau's speciality. In 2002, he took over a smithy dating back to 1926. Since then, his Berlin-based company has created everything from door handles for the Adlon luxury hotel to gates for Berlin's Bode Museum.

For Eisenzahn 1, Fittkau and his team created the 3.7-metre-high front door, along with smaller versions that leads to the courtyard. "The substantial porch canopy, a common feature in Paris around 1900, was a technical challenge – we used 3D structural engineering software. There are a lot more regulations now than there were 100-odd years ago", Fittkau says. The tools, though, have hardly changed: hammer, anvil, tongs, forge coke, flypress. For the perimeter fence over 100 decorative pieces, flourishes that recall branches, were crafted by hand. Their creation required the utmost care – once put together, the pieces needed to add up to a flawless design, which meant working to tolerances of just a few millimetres. The fitting of those heavy doors, yet another occasion for that combination of brawn and dexterity, was a great moment – and a symbolic one too. After all, a front door marks the point at which a building becomes a home.

RS

*Rund zwei Wochen arbeitete man an Flügeln,
Rahmen und Oberlichtern, die dann in
elegantem Schwarz lackiert und eingebaut wurden*

*The doors, frame and top lights took
around two weeks to make and were then painted
in elegant black and installed*

Seit Jahrhunderten bewährtes Werkzeug
für den weißen Werkstoff, dessen kapriziöse
Trocknungszeiten man einst durch Beimischen
von Leimwasser, Milch oder Zucker
verzögerte – sowie von Bier und Wein!

Tools such as these have been used to make
mouldings for centuries. The plaster mix itself
is capricious stuff; in the past, everything
from limewater to milk, sugar and
even beer or wine was added to delay drying

Jedes Profil ist 2,50 m lang, gut 400 Stück
wurden in der Werkstatt in Alt-Hohenschönhausen gefertigt. Dicht an dicht hingen
sie von Deckenschienen und warteten
darauf, zum Kurfürstendamm transportiert
und sorgsam angedübelt zu werden

Each moulding is 2.5 m long; around
400 were made by Ulrich Jacobi's Berlin firm.
Here, they hang side by side from
overhead rails, waiting to be transported

Abgüsse historischer Rosetten und überbordender
Schmuckelemente zieren die Werkstattwände bei der
Berliner Stuckmanufaktur Jacobi – davor fertigt
eine Mitarbeiterin in vielen Arbeitsgängen Profile

Casts of historic roses and elaborate ornaments
decorate the workshop walls at Jacobi Stuck –
in the foreground, an employee creates plaster
mouldings, a process that has many separate stages

*In der Spandauer Werkstatt von Pergande Treppen, familiengeführt in dritter Generation, wurden die Wangen vorgefertigt; der Einbau der 22-stufigen Treppe erfolgte vor Ort in der Maisonette von Eisenzahn 1*

*Stringers being prefabricated at the workshop of stair makers Pergande, a third-generation family firm. The 22-step staircase was then installed on site in the Eisenzahn 1 maisonette*

*Die Wangen der Treppe werden in der Werkstatt mittels sogenannter Igel perfekt in Form gebogen, später halten sie die Trittstufen. Zugrunde liegen präzise Pläne*

*Before installation, the stair stringers into which the treads will later be fixed are bent into the required shape, as specified in detailed designs*

„*Jeder Stamm, der verarbeitet wird, fällt in Farbe und Struktur anders aus – ein Beweis für die Unverwechselbarkeit des Materials*"

"*No two trunks are identical in colour and structure, demonstrating the individuality of this raw material*"

# AT A GLANCE: STAIRCASES

SIE FÜHREN ELEGANT DURCHS HAUS ODER VERBINDEN SCHWUNG-
VOLL DIE ETAGEN EINER WOHNUNG: *TREPPENUNIKATE*, IN HANDARBEIT
AUS HOLZ GEZIMMERT ODER MIT NOBLEN NATURSTEINEN BELEGT

---

ELEGANTLY LINKING THE FLOORS OF A HOUSE OR THE STOREYS OF
A DUPLEX APARTMENT, THESE STAIRCASES ARE HAND-BUILT ONE-OFFS
CRAFTED FROM WOOD OR FINISHED WITH FINE NATURAL STONE

DÜSSELDORF, CARMENSTRASSE

*Stadtresidenz: Das charmante Townhouse-
Duo in Oberkassel mit drei Geschossen
entwarf Sebastian Treese (2015)*

*Staircase from a pair of charming
three-storey townhouses in Oberkassel,
designed by Sebastian Treese (2015)*

DÜSSELDORF, LINDENSTRASSE

*Klassisch: halbhohe Wandvertäfelungen,
dezente Stuckprofile und ein Schachbrett-
boden von zeitloser Schönheit (2012)*

*Wainscoting, subtle plasterwork and
a timelessly elegant chequerboard
floor add up to a classic look (2012)*

BERLIN, HAUS FRIEDRICH

*Grunewald-Grandezza: Am Goldfink-
weg schraubt sich dieser stilvollendete
Treppenaufgang empor (2014)*

*All the grandeur of Grunewald –
a supremely elegant winding
staircase on Goldfinkweg (2014)*

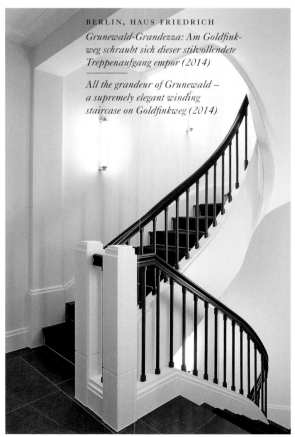

DÜSSELDORF, SOPHIENHOF

*Trikolore: Der Läufer in klassisch-klarem
Rot frischt das sich sonst zurückhaltende
Treppenhaus kongenial auf (2008)*

*Tricolour triumph: a simple runner in
classic red brilliantly brightens up an
otherwise restrained staircase (2008)*

BERLIN, WISSMANNSTRASSE

*Lightshow: Klug platzierte Appliken
streuen helle Akzente, die das Kantige des
Treppengeländers betonen (2017)*

*Light show: carefully placed sconces cast
striking patterns that emphasise
the angularity of the banister (2017)*

KEMPEN, KLOSTERSTRASSE

*Verneigung vor der Formensprache der Vergangenheit: In der Stadtvilla vereinen sich Klassik, Komfort und Stil (2013)*

*Classicism, convenience and style are combined in a villa that pays tribute to aesthetic traditions of the past (2013)*

BERLIN, NIKISCHSTRASSE

*Denkmal reloaded: Das Landhaus Pinn von 1923 wurde behutsam vom Ballast zahlreicher Bausünden befreit (2012)*

*Much disfigured since it was built in 1923, Landhaus Pinn has now been meticulously restored (2012)*

DÜSSELDORF, BANKSTRASSE

*Urban Chic: In exzellenter Metropolenlage entwarf RKW 16 Wohnungen; beide Treppenhäuser gestaltete Oliver Jungel (2013)*

*Our 16-unit, RKW-designed development close to the city centre boasts a pair of staircases by Oliver Jungel (2013)*

BERLIN, GRIEGSTRASSE

*Townhouse-Grazie: Das Stadthaus mit gut 280 qm Wohnfläche und sein Zwilling nebenan strahlen urbane Gediegenheit aus (2012)*

*Offering 280 sqm of living space, this stunning townhouse (one of a pair) is the epitome of urbane elegance (2012)*

DÜSSELDORF, NEANDERHOF

*Feinfühlig: Zurückgenommene Tonalität trifft auf wertige Materialien – eine Stilgleichung, die diskrete Ästhetik garantiert (2010)*

*Tonal understatement and first-class materials come together in a design of subtle sophistication (2010)*

# REPORT: FANTASTIC FLOOR PLANS

Ralf Schmitz und Axel Martin Schmitz im Gespräch über wechselnde *Lebensgewohnheiten, Raumfolgen* – und Sensibilität für *Abstellflächen*

Ralf Schmitz and Axel Martin Schmitz discuss *layouts, lifestyle changes* – and the importance of *storage spaces*

FOTOS **GREGOR HOHENBERG** INTERVIEW **CHRISTIAN TRÖSTER**

*Wir sitzen hier im Konferenzraum am Stammsitz des Unternehmens in Kempen. Seit 1864 steht Ihr Familienname für Baukultur – seit wann beschäftigen Sie beide sich mit Grundrissen?*

RALF SCHMITZ: Ich kenne das Thema schon von Kindheit an durch meinen Vater, später bin ich selbst Immobilienentwickler geworden. Aber es gab doch eine Zäsur in meiner Arbeit Ende der Neunziger: Da habe ich angefangen, mehr auf traditionelle Architektur zu setzen. Damit war auch ein tiefgreifender innerer Wandel verbunden. Die Wohnungen wurden größer, wir achteten nun auf Sichtachsen und inszenierte Raumfluchten, sogenannte Enfiladen. Die Bereiche Kochen, Essen, Wohnen und das Kaminzimmer wurden durch zweiflügelige Türen verbunden. Und das Entree erfuhr eine Aufwertung: Wer in die Wohnung kommt, der kann gleich durch eine Glastür auf ein schönes Möbel oder einen Kamin schauen. Das alles war neu für uns – doch wir hatten damit sofort Erfolg.

AXEL MARTIN SCHMITZ: Es ist bis heute ein großer Unterschied zu den Wettbewerbern, dass wir den Grundrissen einen hohen Stellenwert einräumen. Auch zulasten der Baukosten: Denn um besondere und individuelle Grundrisse zu erreichen, gehen wir beim Schallschutz und der Leitungsführung auch

*Ralf Schmitz stellte die Firma seines Urgroßvaters neu auf, 2011 stieg sein Sohn Axel Martin ins Unternehmen ein ——— Two generations of expertise: Ralf Schmitz relaunched his great-grandfather's firm; his son Axel Martin came on board in 2011*

unkonventionelle Wege. Standard wäre es, Küchen und Bäder um die Treppenhauskerne und die Steigestränge der Leitungen und Rohre drum herum zu organisieren. Wir machen es aber oft anders.

*Also ist Ihr Vorgehen nicht technikgetrieben, sondern orientiert sich an den Bedürfnissen und Wünschen der Bewohner?*
RALF SCHMITZ: Genau. Der Grundriss hat Priorität, nicht die vermeintliche Rationalität der Konstruktion. Wir fragen: Wer will da leben, wie will er leben, was ist in dieser Lage für ihn der perfekte Grundriss? Es ist die Aufgabe der Technik, das zu ermöglichen; die Technik soll dienen, nicht bestimmen. Das kann man so allerdings nur im oberen Preissegment machen.

AXEL MARTIN SCHMITZ: Wir haben in den vergangenen zehn Jahren nicht einen Steigestrang einfach so von oben bis unten durchs Haus gezogen. Das hat auch Auswirkungen auf die Statik. Wir müssen manchmal massive und kostspielige Unterzüge einbauen. Andere würden sagen, das sei es nicht wert.

*Was ist der Mehrwert in den Grundrissen durch all den technischen und organisatorischen Aufwand?*
AXEL MARTIN SCHMITZ: Seit unserer Hinwendung zur klassischen Architektur arbeiten wir an dem Thema „Durchwohnen", daran, dass eine Wohnung Fenster an zwei gegenüberliegenden Seiten des Hauses hat. Außerdem ist uns wichtig, unterschiedliche Grundrisse innerhalb eines Gebäudes realisieren zu können. Wir haben selten zwei identische Wohnungen in einem Haus – sogar bei 30 Einheiten und mehr.

*Das ist das Gegenteil von seriellem Bauen und die größtmögliche Annäherung einer Wohnung an eine individuell geplante Villa.*
AXEL MARTIN SCHMITZ: In unserer Haltung bezüglich der Grundrisse sind wir so ähnlich wie der Vatikan: prinzipientreu. Da reagiert man lieber ein bisschen zu spät auf die Entwicklungen der Zeit, als dass man sich in Tagestrends vergaloppiert. Es bedarf keiner dramatisch-modischen Gesten, um Qualität zu erzeugen. Wir bieten eine gewisse Bandbreite von Grundrissen, aber alle unsere Häuser haben eine Seele – sie sind mehr als einfach nur ein Dach überm Kopf. Der Grundriss soll abbilden, dass die Menschen hier wirklich leben und nicht nur eingezogen sind.

*In der modernen Architektur bis in die Achtziger hinein hatten Räume oft eindimensionale Funktionszuweisungen: Wohnraum, Elternschlafzimmer, Kind, Kind. Solche Einheiten waren später für*

*Wohngemeinschaften oder auch das freiberufliche Arbeiten zuhause nicht zu gebrauchen. Altbauwohnungen aus der Gründerzeit dagegen können sich auch neuen Bedürfnissen gut anpassen. Wie wirkt sich das bei Ihren Grundrissen aus?*
RALF SCHMITZ: Bei Wohnungen mit großen Grundflächen, wie wir sie bauen, wird man nie eine zu enge Funktionalität finden. Unsere Küchen sind natürlich zum Kochen da, aber dort kann noch jemand helfen oder zuschauen und plaudern. Und man kann dort auch zusammen essen. Ebenso unsere Bäder: Sie haben eine Größe, die es erlaubt, noch einen Sitz oder eine Liege hineinzustellen – keine Waschkammern, wo die einzige Gestaltungsmöglichkeit ein Frotteevorleger ist. Wir nennen auch keinen Raum „Kinderzimmer", sondern „Schlafzimmer 2" oder „Schlafzimmer 3". Diese sind aber von der Größe stets so, dass sie sich auch zum Beispiel als Bibliothek oder Gästezimmer nutzen lassen.

## „WIR HABEN SELTEN ZWEI IDENTISCHE WOHNUNGEN IN EINEM HAUS, SOGAR BEI 30 EINHEITEN UND MEHR."

*Die Variabilität der Nutzung resultiert aus der Grundfläche?*
AXEL MARTIN SCHMITZ: Nicht nur. Wir haben über die Jahrzehnte eine sehr genaue Vorstellung davon bekommen, was gut angenommen wird.

*Und das wäre?*
RALF SCHMITZ: Wichtig ist zum Beispiel ein am Wohnzimmer gelegener Raum von um die sieben Quadratmeter, mit offenem Durchgang. Diese kleine Fläche kommt wirklich gut an. Viele nutzen sie als Arbeitsbereich oder dort steht der Fernseher.

AXEL MARTIN SCHMITZ: Zum Thema „Grundriss" gehört auch das sogenannte Elektrogespräch. Das klingt zwar zunächst erst mal unspannend, aber die Entscheidung darüber, wo im Haus der Fernseher steht, hat Einfluss auf vieles andere. Unsere Kunden sind aber keine homogene Gruppe. Für manche ist ein Hauswirtschaftsraum wichtig, für andere nicht – das hängt übrigens auch von der Lage ab. Ähnliches gilt für die Küche. Es gibt Menschen, für die ist eine offene Küche unmöglich wegen der Gerüche. Während für andere der wichtigste Teil von Geselligkeit nicht das Essen ist, sondern das gemeinsame Kochen.

*Darin klingt ein Grundthema des Wohnens an: das Verhältnis von Gemeinschaft und Privatheit. Bei dem eben schon erwähnten Annex zum Wohnzimmer zum Beispiel möchte man für sich sein, aber nicht isoliert. Andere Teile der Wohnung dagegen gelten als Privatissimum und werden separiert.*

AXEL MARTIN SCHMITZ: Ja, das ist bei uns sehr deutlich. Es kann nicht passieren, dass ein Gast versehentlich ins Masterbad oder das große Schlafzimmer stolpert. Denn auch Leute, die gerne Gäste haben, möchten einen Teil ihres Lebens wirklich privat halten.

*Das Exterieur Ihrer Häuser orientiert sich oft an klassischen Bauweisen, aber auch die Innenausstattung, etwa mit Stuckprofilen. Doch einen gründerzeitlichen Berliner Grundriss mit langem Flur und der Küche am hinteren Ende der Wohnung wird man bei Ihnen trotzdem nicht finden, oder?*

RALF SCHMITZ: Das kann man so sagen. Mit Raumhöhen und Stuck wird die Anmutung eines alten Hauses geboten. Aber natürlich gab es früher keine Küche, die ans Ess- und Wohnzimmer angegliedert war. Die Grundrisse von damals waren nicht effizient nach heutigen Maßstäben. Und die Lebensverhältnisse haben sich geändert. Bei meinen Eltern verbrachte man den Abend im Wohnzimmer, bei meinem Sohn sitzen heute alle an einem langen Esstisch. Ähnliche Veränderungen sehe ich bei Küchen und Kinderzimmern. In meinem Elternhaus, das ziemlich groß war, gab es nur eine reine Arbeitsküche. Wir wären nie auf die Idee gekommen, jemandem Gesellschaft zu leisten, der in der Küche hantiert. Und mein Kinderzimmer war geradezu spartanisch, nur zehn Quadratmeter groß – an ein eigenes Bad war sowieso nicht zu denken. Heute ist das bei unseren Grundrissen immer dabei.

## „AUCH MENSCHEN, DIE GERNE GÄSTE HABEN, MÖCHTEN EINEN TEIL IHRES LEBENS WIRKLICH PRIVAT HALTEN."

*Inwieweit beeinflusst die äußere Gestalt des Gebäudes den Grundriss?*
RALF SCHMITZ: Äußere Form und Grundriss müssen in einem guten Verhältnis zueinander stehen. Unsere Architekten wissen, dass sich die Grundrisse der Fassadenästhetik nicht unterordnen sollen. Für den Wohnkomfort nehmen wir an der Rückfassade auch mal eine Asymmetrie in Kauf, etwa wenn Brüstungen in der Küche etwas höher angelegt werden. So kann man Herd oder Spüle vor dem Fenster platzieren!

AXEL MARTIN SCHMITZ: Auch bei solchen Entscheidungen verstehen wir uns als Vertreter unserer Kunden. Für sie denken wir mit und voraus. Wir haben die Erfahrung, speziell für solche Details. Ähnliches gilt für nötige Abstellräume und Abstellflächen.

RALF SCHMITZ: Ich habe schon vor langer Zeit eine Liste gemacht, wie viele laufende Meter an Abstellflächen bei bestimmten Wohnungsgrößen vorhanden sein müssen. Das wird von den Architekten öfter nicht berücksichtigt. Wenn das der Fall ist, bestehen wir darauf, dass sie umplanen. Architekten haben für Abstellräume und -flächen weniger Sensibilität.

---

*We're sitting in your conference room in Kempen, the town where your family-run firm has its headquarters. How long have floor plans been a part of your own life?*
RALF SCHMITZ: They are something I first became aware of as a kid, thanks to my father. Then I went on to become a property developer myself. There was a turning point in my work in the late 1990s though, when I started to focus more on traditional architecture. With this switch came far-reaching internal changes. Our apartments got larger, we started considering sight lines and creating suites of rooms, which are known as enfilades. We linked kitchen, dining and living areas via double doors. And the hall was given more weight so that, when someone enters the apartment, they can immediately look through a glass door towards an attractive piece of furniture or a fireplace. All this took us into new territory – and also brought us immediate success.

AXEL MARTIN SCHMITZ: It's still a key point of difference between us and our competitors that we attach a lot of importance to floor plans – even if that increases building costs. To create floor plans that are individual and special, we sometimes have to take an unconventional approach to noise insulation as well as to wiring and plumbing. Here, the norm is to organise kitchens and bathrooms around the stairwells and the risers for the electrics and heating, but we often deviate from that.

*So your approach is driven not by technical requirements but by the wants and needs of the occupants?*
RALF SCHMITZ: Exactly. The floor plan has absolute priority, not the supposed construction logic. We ask ourselves: Who will want to live there? What kind of lifestyle will they have? And what is the perfect floor plan for them and their lifestyle? A building's technical services need to facilitate this; they

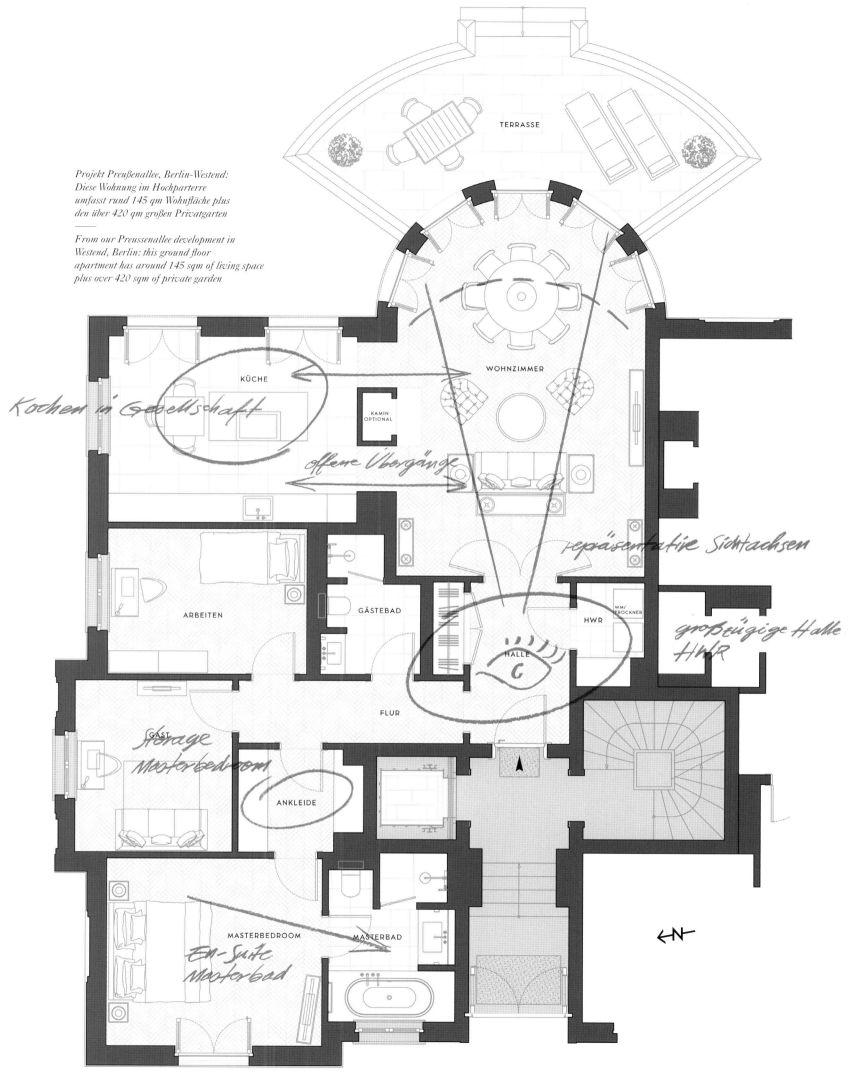

*Projekt Preußenallee, Berlin-Westend:
Diese Wohnung im Hochparterre
umfasst rund 145 qm Wohnfläche plus
den über 420 qm großen Privatgarten*

*From our Preussenallee development in
Westend, Berlin: this ground floor
apartment has around 145 sqm of living space
plus over 420 sqm of private garden*

TERRASSE

WOHNZIMMER

KÜCHE

Kochen in Gesellschaft

KAMIN
OPTIONAL

offene Übergänge

repräsentative Sichtachsen

ARBEITEN

GÄSTEBAD

HWR

WM/
TROCKNER

großzügige Halle
HWR

HALLE

FLUR

GAST

Storage
Masterbedroom

ANKLEIDE

MASTERBEDROOM

MASTERBAD

En-Suite
Masterbad

N

65

should serve, not dictate. It's an approach that's only feasible at the higher end of the market.

AXEL MARTIN SCHMITZ: In the past ten years, we haven't put in a single riser that just went straight up through the house. That has consequences for the structural engineering though – sometimes we have to put in heavy, expensive joists. Others would argue that it's not worth doing.

*Given the technical and organisational complexity, how do such floor plans add value?*
AXEL MARTIN SCHMITZ: Since we started focusing on classically designed architecture, we have been working to make sure each apartment has windows on two opposite sides of the building. It's also important to us that apartments within the same building have different floor plans. We rarely have two identical apartments in a block – even in those of 30 units or more.

## "WE RARELY HAVE TWO IDENTICAL APARTMENTS IN A BLOCK – EVEN IN THOSE OF 30 UNITS OR MORE."

*That's the polar opposite of standardised construction and as close as you can get to apartments built like individually planned villas.*
AXEL MARTIN SCHMITZ: In our approach to floor plans, we're a bit like the Vatican – we stick to our principles. We would rather be a little slow in reacting to contemporary developments than get sidetracked by day-to-day trends. You don't need eye-catching on-trend gestures to produce something of quality. We offer a certain spectrum of floor plans, but each of our buildings has a soul – they are more than just a roof over your head. The floor plan should reflect the fact that the apartments' occupants aren't just moving in, they're setting up home.

*Up until the 1980s, modern homes tended to give rooms clearly defined roles: living area, parents' bedroom, children's bedrooms. This subsequently made them ill-suited to the needs of house-sharers or home-workers. Apartments developed in the late 19th century, on the other hand, are better able to adapt to these new requirements. How is that reflected in your own floor plans?*
RALF SCHMITZ: With the kind of large floor areas our apartments have, you don't get that sort of over-narrow definition of roles. Our kitchens are of course for cooking, but they also allow others to lend a hand, watch or chat – and have space for people to eat together. It's a similar picture with our bathrooms: they are big enough to accommodate a chair or a recliner – these are not washrooms in which the only scope for decoration is the addition of a terry bathmat. And we don't label any of our rooms "children's bedrooms", we prefer to say bedroom 2 or 3, but such spaces are always of a size that allows them to be used as a library or guest bedroom instead.

*So flexibility in usage is a consequence of the floor area?*
AXEL MARTIN SCHMITZ: Among other things. Over the decades we have gained a very precise idea of what features go down well.

*And they are?*
RALF SCHMITZ: It's important, for instance, to have a separate area of around seven square metres adjacent to and open to the living room. This space is really popular with clients. Some use it as a study, others put the television there.

AXEL MARTIN SCHMITZ: Another aspect of the floor plan is the electronics. It might not be the most exciting topic, but the decision as to where to put the television in your new home affects many other things. Our clients are not a homogenous group however. A utility room is important to some but not to others – something that also varies from location to location by the way. It's a similar story with kitchens. There are those for whom open-plan kitchens are a no-no because of the smells, but, for others, cooking together is a more important social occasion than the dinner itself.

*This touches on a key domestic theme: the relationship between shared and private spaces. Those using the aforementioned living room annexe, for instance, want space to themselves but not to shut themselves away. Other areas of the home, on the other hand, are private sanctuaries and thus separated off.*
AXEL MARTIN SCHMITZ: Yes, our homes very much emphasise that. They make sure a guest can't accidentally walk into the master bathroom or the main bedroom. After all, even those who like having people round want to keep parts of their lives private.

*The exteriors of your buildings often take their cue from classical architecture, as do interior features such as plaster mouldings. But that doesn't mean apartments have the kind of plan that prevailed in the late 19th century, with long halls and kitchens towards the back?*

*In der Berliner Niederlassung am Kurfürstendamm besprechen Ralf und Axel Martin Schmitz ausführlich die Grundrisse eines neuen Projekts* —— *At the company's Berlin base, Ralf and Axel Martin Schmitz discuss the floorplans of a new project*

RALF SCHMITZ: That's right. The high ceilings and plaster mouldings help to create the look and feel you get in older properties but the latter, of course, never had kitchens that adjoined the living/dining areas. From a contemporary perspective, the floor plans of those days are inefficient. And people's lifestyles have changed. At my parents', evenings were spent in the living room; at my son's, everyone sits around a long dining table. I've seen a similar change with kitchens and children's bedrooms as well. At the house I grew up in, which was quite a big house, the kitchen was just for working in. If someone was busy in the kitchen, it would never have occurred to us to keep them company. And my childhood bedroom was positively spartan, measuring just ten square metres – and there was never any question of having a separate bathroom. Now, though, it's a given with our floor plans.

## "EVEN THOSE WHO LIKE HAVING PEOPLE ROUND WANT TO KEEP PARTS OF THEIR LIVES PRIVATE."

*To what extent does the exterior influence the floor plan?*
RALF SCHMITZ: Exterior design and floor plan have to work well together. It's a recurring theme that our architects want to put the aesthetics of the façade before the floor plans. That's something we can't allow. We're happy to accept asymmetry in a rear-facing façade if it improves the residents' living experience – we might position the sills in the kitchen slightly higher, for instance, because this allows a sink or cooker to be placed in front of the window.

AXEL MARTIN SCHMITZ: Here, too, we see ourselves as representatives of our clients. We plan intelligently and plan ahead – we have a wealth of experience, especially when it comes to such details. That goes for storage areas and spaces too.

RALF SCHMITZ: I have a list I drew up a long time ago noting how many linear metres of storage space you need for various sizes of apartment. It's something architects are sometimes prone to forget. If they do, we insist that they redraw the plans. Architects have lesser appreciation of storage spaces and areas.

# RENDERING & REALITY

VISUALISIERUNGEN DER ARCHITEKTUREN
VON RALF SCHMITZ SIND *FASZINIERENDE ILLUSIONEN* –
DENN DIE FERTIGEN BAUWERKE ENTSPRECHEN
PERFEKT IHREM AM COMPUTER ENTSTANDENEN BILD

A TRICK OF THE EYE? SO CONVINCING
ARE *THE VISUALISATIONS* OF RALF SCHMITZ'S
ARCHITECTS, IT CAN BE HARD TO TELL
COMPUTER IMAGE AND BUILT WORK APART

RENDERINGS **SEBASTIAN TREESE**    FOTOS **GREGOR HOHENBERG, RALPH RICHTER**    TEXT **INA MARIE KÜHNAST**

*Berlin-Wilmersdorf: Noch eine halb fertige
Computervision in Cinema 4D, bald ein
prächtiger Bau aus Backstein: Beim
Ludwigkirchplatz entstehen ab 2019
über 40 repräsentative Wohneinheiten
in der Emser Straße*

*Berlin-Wilmersdorf: Now a half-finished
rendering in Cinema 4D, soon to be a handsome
brick façade: work on this development of
over 40 units on Emser Strasse begins in 2019*

*Wissmannstraße, Berlin-Grunewald (2017):*
*Nur die Vorgartenmauer ist nun anders geworden –*
*nämlich aus lokaltypischem Backstein,*
*so wie die des Nachbarn in der Villenkolonie*

—

*Wissmannstrasse, Berlin (2017): only the front*
*garden's wall is different, having been built in the*
*area's trademark red brick to match its neighbour*

74

*Eisenzahn 1, Berlin (2016): Wie eineiige Zwillinge wirken die von Hand stuckierten Fassaden des prächtigen Baus beim Kurfürstendamm – die rechte ist die echte*

*Eisenzahn 1, Berlin (2016): the two front elevations of this magnificent building off Kurfürstendamm could be identical twins –the real façade is the one on the right*

„Der Betrachter wird auf feine Details
aufmerksam, die Atmosphäre erzeugen"

"Fine details that create an ambience are called
to the observer's attention"

*Berlin-Grunewald: Gleich am Forst steht Haus*
*Friedrich im Goldfinkweg (links der Entwurf)*

*Berlin-Grunewald: Haus Friedrich, a villa right*
*by the eponymous forest (left: its rendering)*

Carmenstraße, Düsseldorf-Oberkassel (2016): per Grafiksoftware (oben) und
vollendet —— Carmenstraße, Düsseldorf (2016): as a computer-generated image (above) and finished

Ein jeder, der sie betrachtet, erliegt ihrer Täuschung. Ist die Wolke am Himmel echt, also ein Foto? Oder doch am Bildschirm entstanden? Und was ist mit dem Laub auf dem Bürgersteig, dem charmanten Oldtimer vor dem Haus? Man möchte sich fast die Augen reiben, so gestochen real wirken gekonnte Visualisierungen.

Die gezeichnete Welt, die hohe Kunst der Illusion, übt seit jeher eine große Faszination auf ihre Betrachter aus. Bereits im 5. Jahrhundert v. Chr. sollen Maler auf einem Wandbild Trauben so täuschend echt dargestellt haben, dass Vögel nach den 2-D-Früchten pickten. Aber auch gezeichnete Architekturwelten blicken auf eine lange Tradition zurück. In der zweiten Hälfte des Barocks trugen Architekten wie Piranesi dazu bei, dass die malerischen Qualitäten ihrer Zeichnungen in Konkurrenz zur Malerei traten.

Aber was steckt hinter der illusionistischen Architekturdarstellung von heute? In erster Linie dient sie dem Entwerfer als Modell, so wie einst die klassische Zeichnung, denn mit jeder Verbildlichung gibt man künftigen Eigentümern ein Versprechen: Dass sie schon lange vor Fertigstellung der Immobilie wissen, wie diese aussehen wird.

Eine Architekturvisualisierung kann jedoch noch viel mehr: Der Betrachter wird auf feine Details aufmerksam, die Atmosphäre erzeugen und ein Gefühl für das Gebäude schaffen. Er kann sich vorstellen, Teil der Szenerie zu werden. Allerdings erfordert diese komplexe Bild-Erstellung ein großes technisches Können, zudem sollte man kompositorische und kunsthistorische Zusammenhänge beherrschen. Im besten Falle kommt dann etwas heraus, das auch losgelöst vom eigentlichen Sujet – der Darstellung des ungebauten Entwurfs – eigenständig, schön und vor allem authentisch ist.

All dies schafft nur eine gelungene Visualisierung. Sie steht für die persönliche Handschrift und Sprache des Architekten und des Bauträgers. In ihrer herausragenden Qualität spiegelt sich auch die Qualität des Bauvorhabens wider. Zudem hat sie der klassischen Handzeichnung voraus, dass bestimmte Aspekte des Entwurfs am noch imaginären Bau besonders veranschaulicht werden können. Naturalistisch visualisiert lassen sich Perspektiven, Raumfolgen oder die Einpassung des Entwurfs in seine Umgebung wiederholt überprüfen und gegebenenfalls verbessern. Die Ästhetik guter Renderings beeinflusst sogar die Architekturfotografie, die sich vermehrt an Visualisierungen orientiert und die Unterschiede zwischen fiktiv und faktisch immer mehr verschwimmen lässt.

Aber zurück zum Versprechen: Wenn man Fiktion perfekt in gebaute Realität umsetzt, dann hat man sein Wort als Bauträger mehr als gehalten, oder? Schauen Sie ganz genau hin!

---

Photograph or computer-generated image? It can be almost impossible to tell the difference. Is that an actual cloud? And what about the leaves on the pavement, or the classic car parked out front? Professional renderings look so real, so convincing, they can have you rubbing your eyes in disbelief. The world of visualisations and illusions has long held a particular fascination. As early as the 5th century BC, skilled artists were said to have painted a mural whose grapes were so lifelike that birds attempted to pick the two-dimensional fruit. Architectural visualisations, too, have a long tradition, especially in the Late Baroque.

What, then, of today's architectural illusions? As with traditional technical drawings, their primary purpose is to model the author's plans and to thus serve as a form of customer guarantee – a guarantee that buyers know, long before completion, what they are getting. But they have other benefits too: they can also be used to draw attention to subtle details that add character and to give a feel for the overall design, allowing would-be owners to picture themselves in the visualised scene.

Generating such complex images, however, requires a high degree of technical skill as well as an understanding of various compositional and art historical aspects. Done well, they have an appeal that goes beyond their actual purpose – the depiction of an as-yet-unbuilt design – with a character, aesthetic quality and, above all, authenticity that is all their own. Such highly accomplished renderings not only faithfully convey the signature style and formal language of the architect and developer, they also reflect the exceptional quality buyers can expect from the finished property.

Compared to hand-drawn visualisations, they have the advantage of enabling certain aspects of the design to be highlighted in a naturalistic fashion, meaning perspectives, layouts and the integration within the surroundings can be checked again and again and improved where necessary. The aesthetic of high-quality renderings has even impacted on architectural photography, thus blurring the lines between the envisaged and the actual even further.

If reality mirrors the rendering, then the developer has surely delivered exactly what they promised. See for yourself!

RS

*Kentenich Hof, Düsseldorf-Golzheim: Die
extravagante Fassade ist reizvolle Zierde der
Gerhard-Domagk-Straße – Art déco als Plan
(oben) und in fertiger Perfektion (rechts)*

*Kentenich Hof, Düsseldorf-Golzheim:
An Art Deco vision (above) and its flawless
realisation (right) – flamboyant curves
catch the eye on Gerhard-Domagk-Strasse*

„Der Betrachter kann sich vorstellen,
Teil der Szenerie zu werden"

_"Renderings allow viewers to picture
themselves in the visualised scene"_

# REPORT: HEADQUARTERS & COMPANY BASES

An *vier Standorten* führt einer der führenden deutschen Projektentwickler für luxuriöse Wohnimmobilien vor, dass der hohe Anspruch auch die *eigene Arbeitswelt* umfasst

With its *four offices* across Germany, RALF SCHMITZ shows that the high standards it applies to property development extend to *its own workspaces* too

FOTOS **RALPH RICHTER, GREGOR HOHENBERG, STEFAN MÜLLER**   TEXT **EVA ZIMMERMANN**

Das Baudenkmal von 1902 in Oberkassel dient seit 2014 als Düsseldorfer Niederlassung des Unternehmens ——— *This historic villa was built in 1902 and has been home to the firm's Düsseldorf offices since 2014*

Schon die Wahl der Firmensitze zeigt, dass sich RALF SCHMITZ dem Zeitlos-Klassischen verpflichtet hat. Die inzwischen drei Dependancen und der Stammsitz befinden sich in besonderen, teils denkmalgeschützten Altbauten und verweisen auf die Baukultur als Fundament der Unternehmensphilosophie. Als Stammhaus in Kempen dient seit 1998 die Villa Brandenburg. Das einstige Wohnhaus eines Fabrikanten wurde 1901 am Stadtring errichtet und liegt nahe zum historischen Viehmarkt. Die Sanierung nahm RALF SCHMITZ selbst in die Hand – genau wie die der Düsseldorfer Niederlassung am Kaiser-Friedrich-Ring, die 2014 bezogen wurde: Das Baudenkmal von 1902 markiert den Eingang zum Stadtteil Oberkassel, der zu den begehrten Vierteln der Rheinmetropole gehört.

Am Berliner Kurfürstendamm steht das Haus, in dem das Unternehmen auf zwei Etagen seine Hauptstadt-Dependance führt. Und in Hamburg sitzt RALF SCHMITZ am Neuen Wall, in direkter Nähe zur Binnenalster, wo seit über hundert Jahren eine von Europas prächtigsten Einkaufsstraßen verläuft.

An allen Standorten entwickelt das Unternehmen im Zusammenspiel aus gehobener Form und kunstfertiger Ausführung jenen klassischen Stilkanon weiter, der alle Bau-

*Über den Empfangsraum samt Materialschaukästen wacht das große Auge von Künstlerin Wiebke Siem („Untitled", 2007)* ——— *A large eye by artist Wiebke Siem ("Untitled", 2007) watches over the reception area with its display cases of materials*

projekte prägt – und auch die firmeneigene Arbeitswelt, die der Architekt Oliver Jungel gestaltet. Geschäftsführer Ralf Schmitz kennt den Interior-Designer seit fast 20 Jahren; er beauftragte ihn auch mit der Einrichtung seines Privathauses und ist vom Ergebnis dauerhaft begeistert: „Ich genieße das zeitlos elegante Interieur jeden Tag aufs Neue."

## IN DEN NIEDERLASSUNGEN WIRD JENER STILKANON GEZEIGT, DER ALLE PROJEKTE PRÄGT.

Weil Jungel den Spagat zwischen Klassik und modernem Komfort perfekt beherrscht, gestaltet er fast alle Foyers, Treppenhäuser und Aufzugskabinen der Projekte in Düsseldorf. Diese Bereiche sind – neben den besonderen Exterieurs – das Herausstellungsmerkmal der RALF-SCHMITZ-Architektur. Jungel lässt gerne Elemente des Art déco in seine Gestaltung einfließen, ist ein Meister des Materials und setzt Texturen und Oberflächen, Farben und Naturtöne kunstvoll zueinander in Beziehung. Stattliche Möbel für großzügige Grundrisse und der Anspruch, die perfekte Lösung für jede räumliche Situation zu finden, prägen seine Entwürfe und führen zu einem hohen Anteil von Maßanfertigungen: vom Konferenztisch über Vitrinen bis hin zu Büromöbeln. Ergänzt werden sie mit hochklassigen Textilien und gediegener Beleuchtung. Lüster und Leuchten kommen etwa von Lindsey Adelman und Flos, ergänzendes Mobiliar von Christian Liaigre; die Gardinen sind maßgefertigt.

Der hohe Einrichtungsstandard in den Standorten hat nicht nur die Funktion, jedem Besucher den Qualitätsanspruch des Unternehmens vor Ort zu zeigen. Er ist auch als Dank an die rund 80 Mitarbeiter (Stand: Ende 2017) gedacht. Mit diesem Ansatz erkennt das Traditionsunternehmen an, dass es letztlich von jedem Einzelnen abhängt, ob die Idee einer hochwertigen, überdauernden und menschenfreundlichen Architektur, wie sie der Geschäftsführer Ralf Schmitz vor 40 Jahren als Vision formulierte, immer wieder aufs Neue in die Realität umgesetzt wird. Der Geschäftsführer ist häufig am Berliner Standort anzutreffen, den er leitet.

2007 trat sein Sohn Richard Alexander Schmitz, Diplom-Kaufmann und Jurist (Master of Laws), nach einigen Jahren bei einem Großkonzern in die Geschäftsführung des Unternehmens ein. Er verantwortet standortübergreifend die kauf-

*Am Tresen aus Messing (links) werden in Düsseldorf Kunden empfangen; aus dem Turmzimmer mit gepolsterten Bänken (rechts) hat man freie Sicht auf die Skyline der Stadt* —— *A brass reception desk (left) greets clients in Düsseldorf; the turret room (right) offers unimpeded views of the city skyline*

männischen Bereiche Finanzierung, Rechnungswesen und Controlling von Düsseldorf aus, leitet die Stabsabteilungen Personal und Organisation sowie die Abteilung Akquisition und koordiniert als Sprecher die Arbeit der Geschäftsführung und die Zusammenarbeit mit dem Aufsichtsrat.

Der jüngste Sohn Axel Martin Schmitz, studierter Betriebswirt, ist seit 2011 Mitglied der Geschäftsführung. Er leitet die Projektentwicklung, die Kundenberatung und die Technik in Kempen und Düsseldorf. Zudem verantwortet er standortübergreifend das Asset Management, die IT und das Marketing.

## DAS UNTERNEHMEN WURDE 2013 ZUR GMBH & Co. KGaA UMGEWANDELT, ALLE AKTIEN SIND IM FAMILIENBESITZ.

Neben dem Tagesgeschäft akkommodieren die Standorte reihum einmal im Quartal den Aufsichtsrat, der 2013 entstand, als die Firma zur RALF SCHMITZ GmbH & Co. KGaA umgewandelt wurde; die Aktien sind vollständig im Familienbesitz.

Wenn die Geschäftsführer und Aufsichtsräte jedes Vierteljahr in einem der Konferenzräume Platz nehmen, dann ist ihnen ein gediegenes Ambiente gewiss, in dem es sich konzentriert arbeiten lässt. Und genau das ist es schließlich, was hinter allem steckt: Orte zu schaffen, die jenen, die sie nutzen, einen angemessenen Rahmen bieten und ästhetisch so hochwertig gestaltet sind, dass man sich in ihnen auf das Wesentliche konzentrieren kann. Dabei bildet die Wertschätzung von Mensch, Ressourcen und Kulturgeschichte eine untrennbare Einheit.

———

RALF SCHMITZ's dedication to timeless traditional architecture can be seen not only in every building it develops, but also in the offices from which the firm operates. All four company premises – the headquarters in Kempen, plus the three other regional offices – are located in historic or even listed buildings and attest to the role architectural heritage plays in the firm's philosophy.

Since 1998, the company has been based at Villa Brandenburg, a former industrialist's residence built in 1901 not far from Kempen's historic marketplace. RALF SCHMITZ took charge of the renovation itself – and later did likewise with the building that since 2014 has housed the firm's Düsseldorf offices. Built in 1902 on Kaiser-Friedrich-Ring and nicknamed Brückenschlösschen, it marks the point at which Oberkassel, one of the city's most desirable areas, begins. The company's Berlin offices occupy two floors of a building on the prestigious Kurfürstendamm, while, in Hamburg, RALF SCHMITZ can be found not far from the Inner Alster lake, on Neuer Wall, a street that has for centuries been one of Europe's premier retail locations.

*Blick auf die Büro- und Meeting-Räume im zweiten und vierten Stock am Kurfürstendamm —— Offices and meeting rooms of the firm's Berlin base on the 2nd and 4th floor of this Kurfürstendamm dwelling*

In each of these locations, the firm's synthesis of refined designs and skilful execution draws on and adds to the canon of traditionally inspired forms. It's a synthesis that also informs the various RALF SCHMITZ offices, which have interiors by Oliver Jungel, whom managing director Ralf Schmitz has known for almost 20 years. Schmitz also commissioned the architect and interior designer with the decoration of his own home, which continue to delight him even now: "I appreciate the timelessly elegant interiors every single day."

## IN 2013 RALF SCHMITZ WAS CONVERTED INTO A JOINT STOCK COMPANY (GMBH & CO. KGAA) – ALL SHARES REMAIN IN THE HANDS OF THE FAMILY.

Jungel is particularly adept at balancing classic style and contemporary luxury, which is why the firm entrusts him with the design of almost all its Düsseldorf developments' foyers, staircases and lift compartments. These areas are – alongside exceptional external architecture – what truly sets a SCHMITZ building apart. Jungel, who often incorporates Art Deco influences into his designs, has a masterful way with materials and an eye for artful juxtapositions, be it of textures and finishes or colours and natural shades. Generous floor areas are paired with impressive furnishings, while his pursuit of the perfect solution for every space and situation often results in a high proportion of bespoke designs – for conference tables, glass cabinets or even office furniture. The finishing touch comes courtesy of high-end textiles and lighting, with chandeliers and lamps by the likes of Lindsey Adelman and Flos featured alongside carefully chosen furniture by Christian Liaigre and custom-made curtains.

*Leseecke im Berliner Büro von Geschäftsführer Ralf Schmitz (links); über den maßgefertigten Konferenzmöbeln hängt ein Lüster von Lindsey Adelman ——— Reading area at the Berlin offices of managing director Ralf Schmitz (left); a chandelier by Lindsey Adelman hangs above the custom-made conference furnishings*

*Die Fabrikantenvilla von 1901 mit einem Foyer im englischen Landhausstil ist Stammsitz der Kempener Firma —— Home to the Kempen headquarters of RALF SCHMITZ, this industrialist's villa from 1901 has a foyer in the English country house style*

On top of day-to-day company business, the four office locations also serve in rotation as the venue for quarterly meetings of the supervisory board, which was instituted in 2013 when RALF SCHMITZ was converted into a joint stock company (GmbH & Co. KGaA – all shares remain in the hands of the family).

Whichever conference room they meet in, the various members of the executive and supervisory boards know that an effortlessly refined ambience awaits, one in which company business can be discussed without distraction. Such single-mindedness lies at the heart of all the firm's work: it is, after all, about creating spaces that are perfectly tailored to their purpose and whose understated luxury allows their users to focus on the things that really matter, spaces in which respect for people, a feel for materials and an appreciation of cultural heritage add up to a truly harmonious whole.

In addition to giving clients a taste of the company's commitment to quality, this fastidious approach to workplace interiors is also an expression of how much it values its roughly 80 employees (as of late 2017) – and thus is an acknowledgement of the role each individual plays in the firm's continued ability to realise its managing director's almost 40-year-old vision of high-quality, enduring and people-centred architecture. These days, Ralf Schmitz himself runs the Berlin offices.

In 2007, his son Richard Alexander Schmitz joined the firm's executive board, having previously graduated in business administration and gained a masters in law, then working in a large corporation for a number of years. From his base in Düsseldorf, he is now responsible for corporate finance, accounting and controlling across the company as well as for personnel and organisation and heads the acquisition department. As spokesperson for the executive board, he also coordinates its work and its dealings with the supervisory board.

## IN EACH OF ITS LOCATIONS, THE FIRM DRAWS ON AND ADDS TO THE CANON OF TRADITIONALLY INSPIRED FORMS.

Youngest son Axel Martin Schmitz, also a business administration graduate, joined the executive board in 2011 and is now head of project development, technical services and customer service in Kempen and Düsseldorf. He also has overall responsibility for asset management, IT and marketing across the firm.

# OUTSTANDING APARTMENT HOUSES

STADTVILLEN VON RALF SCHMITZ VEREINEN
ZEITLOSE UND *SCHÖNE ARCHITEKTUREN*, GEPAART
MIT *KOMFORT UND TECHNIK* VON HEUTE

THESE *HANDSOME PROPERTIES* COMBINE
CLASSICALLY STYLED ARCHITECTURE WITH
THE *LUXURIES AND AMENITIES* OF TODAY

FOTOS **GREGOR HOHENBERG, RALPH RICHTER**    TEXT **INA MARIE KÜHNAST**

*Neanderhof, Düsseldorf-Flingern: Eleganz
über fünf Geschosse. Naturstein und Edelstahl
des herrschaftlichen Eingangsportals
vermitteln einen weltstädtischen Charakter*

*Neanderhof, Düsseldorf-Flingern: Five floors of
refined style. Steel accents and natural stone lend
the entrance an air of sophisticated grandeur*

*Haus Weyhe, Berlin-Dahlem: Das klassizistische Mehrfamilienhaus aus rotem Strangpressklinker zieren vier helle ionische Säulen und stuckierte Gesimsbänder*

*Haus Weyhe, Berlin-Dahlem: Clinker bricks plus classical details like pale Ionic columns and plaster cornices adorn the front of this apartment building*

*Haus Battenberg, Düsseldorf-Golzheim: Heller Klinker mit strengen Schmuckelementen und Profilierungen strukturiert die imposante Fassade*

*Haus Battenberg, Düsseldorf-Golzheim: Geometric ornamentation and horizontal mouldings lend a structured look to the pale clinker-brick façade*

*Eisenzahn 1, Berlin-Wilmersdorf: Sanft geschwungene Loggien und Balkone an der Gartenfront des Wohnpalais zeigen die Rückkehr der Belle Époque auf zeitgenössische Art*

*Eisenzahn 1, Berlin-Wilmersdorf: Gently rounded loggias and balconies grace the garden aspect of this palatial property, a contemporary take on the Belle Époque style*

„*An den eleganten Fassaden lässt sich die außergewöhnliche Bauqualität ablesen*"

"*Their timelessly elegant façades speak of exceptional standards of construction quality*"

*Karlshof, Düsseldorf-Oberkassel: Edel und einladend wirkt das großstädtische Wohnensemble aus insgesamt vier Häusern, deren Fassaden historisierende Baudetails schmücken*

*Karlshof, Düsseldorf-Oberkassel: Comprising our apartments with façades featuring historicist details, this ensemble has an exclusive yet inviting look*

*Haus Berengar, Düsseldorf-Oberkassel: Elegant schwingt sich das schmucke Gebäude um die Straßenecke und macht bereits von Ferne durch die aufgesetzte Rotunde auf sich aufmerksam*

*Haus Berengar, Düsseldorf-Oberkassel: This handsome building elegantly follows the street corner's curve and catches the eye from afar with its rooftop rotunda*

Ein Deutscher revolutionierte einst den New Yorker *way of living:* George Henry Griebel entwarf das legendäre „The Dakota", das 1884 am Central Park entstand. Seine Idee, 65 Luxuswohnungen mit bis zu 20 Zimmern in einem einzigen Gebäude zu vereinen, galt als epochal. Denn bis dato lebten vermögende Familien stets in frei stehenden Villen auf großen Grundstücken außerhalb, im turbulenten Zentrum nur eher ärmere Bevölkerungsschichten in Mehrfamilienhäusern. Groß war die Entrüstung der New Yorker, dass zahlreiche Familien der *upper class* komfortabel unter einem Dach leben sollten. Man tuschelte, was in diesem Domizil so alles vor sich gehen würde ...

Noch viel mehr Aufgebrachtheiten bekam Georges-Eugène Haussmann, Präfekt von Paris unter Napoleon III., zu hören, als er ab 1853 mit der radikalen Neuanlage der Seine-Metropole begann. Die Pariser hingen sehr an ihren schmalen, nur selten vielstöckigen Häusern, die die schmalen Gassen der Innenstadt säumten. Im Erdgeschoss lag meist ein Geschäft, die Wohnung des Ladeninhabers direkt darüber. In den übrigen *appartements* lebte die Arbeiterklasse; der Bevölkerungszunahme geschuldet, vermietete man sogar Dachkammern als kostengünstige *studios*. Von Pariser Großbürgertum also – noch – keine Spur. Im neuen Zentrum à la Haussmann wurden dann die Fronten breiter, die Fassaden höher, klassizistisch-homogener und Straßen wie die Rue de Rivoli zum Vorbild für prächtige Boulevards, die bis heute Paris prägen. Das Interesse Haussmanns galt dem architektonischen Gesamtensemble, er vereinheitlichte Material, Dimensionen und bestimmte wiederkehrende Fassadenelemente. Die mittelalterliche Enge wich lichten Alleen mit eleganten Häusern, einem baulichen Spiegelbild der aufkommenden bürgerlichen Gesellschaft.

Der Exkurs in die Geschichte zeigt, wo die schmucken Stadtvillen wie Eisenzahn 1 in Berlin, Haus Battenberg oder der Neanderhof in Düsseldorf ihre Wurzeln haben. Mehrfamilienhäuser von RALF SCHMITZ setzen auf jenen bis heute anziehend wirkenden, traditionellen Charme und zitieren vom Klassizismus bis zum Art déco die Architekturgeschichte. An den eleganten, weltstädtisch anmutenden Fassaden lässt sich die außergewöhnlich hohe bauliche Qualität ablesen. Dennoch passen diese Stadtvillen sich kompromisslos dem zeitgenössischen Lebensstil und Komfort an, ohne in modernistische Trends abzugleiten.

Jedes neu errichtete SCHMITZ-Haus regt die Fantasie seiner Betrachter an: Wie wohnt es sich wohl auf der Beletage des Neanderhofs, welche Epoche inspirierte zur geschwungenen Fassade von Eisenzahn 1, welchen Ausblick genießt man von der Dachterrasse? Die fein abgestimmten Gesamtkunstwerke aus Bau, Umgebung und Ausstattung versprühen die Magie ihrer architektonischen Vorbilder an berühmten Avenues und Boulevards dieser Welt und spannen gekonnt einen stilistischen Bogen in die Gegenwart.

---

In 1884, a German revolutionised New York living. With his design for the now legendary Dakota building on Central Park, George Henry Griebel set out to combine 65 luxury apartments with up to 20 rooms each under one roof – a then unprecedented idea. Wealthy families had hitherto dwelt in free-standing villas built on large out-of-town plots, while apartment blocks in the city's turbulent centre were the preserve of poorer sections of society. To many New Yorkers, the idea that numerous well-to-do families should live happily within the same building was scandalous, and there was much gossiping about what these occupants might get up to ...

Even greater opprobrium greeted Georges-Eugène Haussmann, prefect of Paris under Napoleon III, when he began his radical reorganisation of the French capital in 1853. People were very fond of the narrow, mostly low-built houses that lined the crowded streets of central Paris. Their ground floors generally contained retail premises, with the shopkeeper living directly above and the remaining flats being occupied by members of the working class. After Haussmann, all that changed. His remodelled city centre featured wider, higher frontages that were more homogenous and classical in style, with roads such as Rue de Rivoli providing the template for the grand boulevards typical of modern-day Paris.

This historical digression outlines where the roots of properties such as Berlin's Eisenzahn 1 or Düsseldorf's Haus Battenberg and Neanderhof lie. The undimmed appeal of the Dakota and of Haussmann's Paris is, after all, one that continues to inform the architecture of our buildings, which draw on traditions from Neoclassicism to Art Deco. From the outside, their timeless façades speak of exceptional standards of build quality, while, inside, their living spaces are perfectly tailored to today's lifestyles yet steer clear of short-lived trends. Every new RALF SCHMITZ development fires the imagination and inspires the curiosity of passers-by. Carefully combining exterior, interior and environment, these aesthetically pleasing properties capture the magic their architectural forebears brought to world-famous avenues and boulevards – and transpose it to the present day.

Parterrassen am Feldmühlepark, Düsseldorf-
Oberkassel: Der Entwurf von RKW setzte auf
Fassadenakzente durch Vor- und Rücksprünge
sowie durch die markante Verkleidung mit
Naturstein, die sich über zwei Geschosse zieht

Parterrassen, Feldmühlepark, Düsseldorf-
Oberkassel: RKW Architekten opted for
façades with recessed and projecting elements plus
a two-storey band of natural stone cladding

*Mannesmannufer, Düsseldorf: Messing und nobler Kohlplatter Muschelkalk dominieren die Front des Hauses. Aus den Wohnungen hat man freie Sicht auf die gesamte Rheinschleife.*

*Mannesmannufer, Düsseldorf: Brass and refined fossiliferous limestone dominate this slender frontage. The apartments within offer unimpeded views of the Rhine*

*Haus Hardenberg, Düsseldorf-Zoo:
Zahlreiche Gauben im Walmdach und
klassische Sprossenfenster verleihen dem
Bau in bester Lage seine freundliche Anmut*

*Haus Hardenberg, Düsseldorf-Zoo:
Numerous dormers and traditional
multi-pane windows lend this Zooviertel
building a friendly look*

*Haus Bahren, Hamburg-Othmarschen:
Erstlingswerk an der Elbe: Das Gebäude von
Kahlfeldt Architekten besticht durch seine
zurückhaltende Architektur- und Formensprache*

*Haus Bahren, Hamburg-Othmarschen:
RALF SCHMITZ goes north. Our first
development in Germany's Elbe city boasts
elegantly understated lines and forms*

99

# AT A GLANCE: LETTERBOXES & BELLS

BAUKUNST ZEIGT SICH AUCH IN DER LIEBE ZUM DETAIL.
KLINGELTABLEAUS UND BRIEFKASTENANLAGEN SOLLEN NICHT
NUR PRAKTISCH SEIN, SONDERN AUCH ELEGANT

THOUGHTFUL ARCHITECTURE IS ABOUT CONSIDERING
EVERY DETAIL. OUR DOORBELL PLATES AND LETTERBOXES
ARE THUS AS ELEGANT AS THEY ARE EASY TO USE

**DÜSSELDORF, MERCATORTERRASSEN**

*Beide Eingangsloggien des U-förmigen
Ensembles zieren großformatige Unterputz-
anlagen aus Edelstahl (2011)*

*Large recessed letterbox units in
stainless steel adorn both entrance porches
at this U-shaped ensemble (2011)*

**DÜSSELDORF, NEANDERHOF**

*Die repräsentative Adresse in Flingern
zeigt sich auch am Glanz der Brief-
stele aus poliertem Edelstahl (2010)*

*A lustrous letterbox unit in polished
stainless steel reflects the prestigious
feel of this building in Flingern (2010)*

**BERLIN, HAUS WEYHE**

*Schön und sicher im Hochparterre: Diskreter
Alarmtransponder in der edlen Klingelplatte
mit Namensgravur (2013)*

*Style and security at ground floor level –
courtesy of an elegant engraved bell board
with discreet alarm transponder (2013)*

**DÜSSELDORF, LANKERSTRSSE**

*Vier Stadtvillen umfasst der klassizierende
Karlshof; integrierte Video-Gegensprechanlagen
verbessern die Sicherheit (2006)*

*Video intercoms offer enhanced security
at our Karlshof development, a
quartet of classically styled villas (2006)*

BERLIN, HUBERTUSGÄRTEN

*Wie ein Kunstwerk wirkt diese noble
Symbiose aus Amerikanischem
Nussbaum und Edelstahlrahmen (2010)*

*American walnut and stainless steel
combine to create letterboxes
that are almost a work of art (2010)*

BERLIN, KURFÜRSTENDAMM

*Das Klingelschild mit erhabenem Logo und
Firmennamen wurde in der Kunstschmiede
Fittkau aus Baubronze angefertigt*

*This sumptuous name and bell plate
was crafted from architectural bronze by
Kunstschmiede Fittkau*

DÜSSELDORF, 22 LUEGALLEE

*Dunkle Grandezza durch lackiertes
Metall für das sorgfältig sanierte Domizil
in Oberkassel (1929 | 2009)*

*Black-painted metal lends a sophisticated
look to this carefully renovated
building in Oberkassel (1929/2009)*

BERLIN, GRIEGSTRASSE

*Edle Bronze, auf Maß in den
Pfosten eingepasst, verleiht der stimmigen
Kombination Noblesse (2012)*

*A made-to-measure bronze panel
adds extra class to this harmonious
gatepost ensemble (2012)*

# REPORT: HOUSE CALL IN DÜSSELDORF

Dr. Jochen Best zog gerade in den *Kentenich Hof* ein.
Der Augenarzt und Richard Alexander Schmitz, Mitgeschäftsführer
des Unternehmens, sprechen über *Stil, Vertrauen und Loyalität*

---

Having just moved into *Kentenich Hof*, ophthalmologist
Dr Jochen Best discusses s*tyle, trust and loyalty*
with company co-director Richard Alexander Schmitz

FOTOS **MAJID MOUSSAVI** INTERVIEW **INA MARIE KÜHNAST**

*Einladend: Zeitgenössische Kunst und exquisiter Naturstein veredeln grafisch elegant das Foyer der Wohneinheit im Zooviertel —— Contemporary art and exquisite natural stone lend an elegant look to the residence's inviting foyer*

*Man betritt bei einem Gebäude von RALF SCHMITZ ein architektonisches und stilistisches Versprechen. Herr Dr. Best, seit über 25 Jahren begeistern Sie sich für diese Baukunst – warum genau?*

DR. JOCHEN BEST: Das beginnt bereits in der großen Lobby eines SCHMITZ-Hauses. Dort sehe ich elegante Lampen neben hochwertigen Holztüren, ein Klingeltableau aus poliertem Messing, dazu geschmackvolles Mobiliar wie eine hübsche Konsole mit feiner Kunst darüber – für mich typisch Schmitz'sche Charakteristika. Ein zurückhaltender Chic ohne laute Accessoires oder bauliche Extravaganzen, die sich schnell überleben. So vollendet sehe ich das anderswo wirklich selten.

*Erinnern Sie sich noch an die Ästhetik früherer RALF-SCHMITZ-Immobilien?*

DR. JOCHEN BEST: Ja, das war Mitte der 80er-Jahre: Zwar konnte ich mir damals als Medizinstudent noch keine RALF-SCHMITZ-Wohnung leisten, habe aber begeistert alle Projekte des Unternehmens verfolgt und mich für ihre Grundrisse und Ausstattung interessiert. Besuche im Düsseldorfer Showroom waren sozusagen ein Hobby von mir. Die waren damals schon wunderschön, aber insgesamt etwas sachlicher und nicht ganz so stilvollendet, wie sie es heute sind.

*Zwei, die sich seit Langem kennen und schätzen: Geschäftsführer Richard Alexander Schmitz (links) und Augenarzt Dr. Jochen Best —— Company co-director Richard Alexander Schmitz (left) and ophthalmologist Dr Jochen Best have long had a great mutual respect*

Großzügige Bäder, tolle Keramik und schickes Parkett wurden bereits verwirklicht. Etwas weniger detailverliebt, aber von unschlagbarer Qualität. Ich würde sagen, dass die stilistische Entwicklung, die sich bis heute vollzogen hat, in Ansätzen bereits sichtbar war, aber was das Unternehmen heute an Immobilien erschafft, begeistert und überrascht mich mit jedem Projekt aufs Neue.

*Herr Schmitz, Ihr Traditionsunternehmen ist in vierter und fünfter Generation familiengeführt. Wie früh ist Ihre Liebe zur Architektur erwacht?*

RICHARD ALEXANDER SCHMITZ: Da sozusagen das Unternehmen stets mit am Esstisch saß und sitzt, als sei es ein Familienmitglied, nimmt es schon eine sehr zentrale Stellung ein. Ich bin also schon als Kind täglich mit Architektur in Berührung gekommen. Meine Eltern sind absolute Ästheten! Qualität und Langlebigkeit sind ihnen immer sehr wichtig gewesen, sodass uns Kinder ihre Philosophie allgegenwärtig umgab. Als Kind und Jugendlicher bei Wochenendausflügen und in Familienurlauben mit meinen Eltern wurde vor interessanten Gebäuden gehalten und es gab kleine Vorträge über den jeweiligen Baustil. Das war immer recht amüsant; wirklich interessant fand ich es erst, als ich älter wurde. Besonders schöne Türen und andere Details, die meinen Eltern auffielen, wurden fotografiert, wanderten dann ins Firmenarchiv und wurden für das eine oder andere Projekt hervorgeholt.

*Herr Dr. Best, schafft es größeres Vertrauen, eine Immobilie bei einem Traditionsunternehmen zu kaufen?*

DR. JOCHEN BEST: Neben der herausragenden Bauqualität ist sicherlich ein wichtiger Faktor, dass RALF SCHMITZ ein Familienunternehmen ist. Ich stamme selbst aus einem solchen und unterstütze solche Firmen natürlich einfach gern als treuer Kunde. Zudem hat man dort feste Ansprechpartner, was beim Kauf einer Immobilie sehr beruhigt – zu wissen, wer der Chef und wer verantwortlich ist, gibt Sicherheit, Vertrauen und das Gefühl von Loyalität, besonders wenn man Geld investiert. Niemand will mit einer halb fertigen Immobilie dastehen, deren Bauträger über alle Berge ist.

*Herr Schmitz, ein Kundenstamm, der sich teilweise über mehrere Generationen hinweg erstreckt, macht sicher stolz. Vor welche Herausforderungen stellt dies Ihr Unternehmen heute, um die Messlatte auch künftig weiter so hoch halten zu können?*

RICHARD ALEXANDER SCHMITZ: Natürlich sind wir sehr glücklich darüber, einen so exzellenten Ruf aufgebaut zu haben – doch ist der bereits ein Verdienst meiner Vorfahren. Für meine Generation geht damit eine große Verantwortung einher, mit der man behutsam umgehen muss. Diesen hohen Anspruch zu halten, ist eine feste Grundeinstellung: Wir geben jeden Tag unser Bestes und wollen uns ständig weiterentwickeln. Das ist wie eine Verfassung, an die wir uns alle halten.

## „WAS DAS UNTERNEHMEN HEUTE AN IMMOBILIEN ERSCHAFFT, BEGEISTERT MICH MIT JEDEM PROJEKT AUFS NEUE."

*Klassische Architekturformen modern eingesetzt, elegante Farbwelten und erlesene Materialien – steigt der eigene Anspruch an eine Immobilie mit dem in Ihrem Fall dritten Erwerb eines RALF-SCHMITZ-Domizils? Beeinflusst es Ihren persönlichen Stil?*

DR. JOCHEN BEST: Definitiv. Man kann ja sehr anschaulich mitverfolgen, wie sich das Unternehmen in den letzten fünf Jahren stilistisch vervollkommnet und Architekturen hervorgebracht hat, in denen vieles stetig verfeinert wurde. Ich habe in bislang drei sehr unterschiedlichen RALF-SCHMITZ-Immobilien gelebt und bin wie ein Zeitzeuge, der diese Veränderungen hautnah miterleben durfte. Es war bereits Wohnen auf hohem Niveau, nun ist es auf höchstem. Das ging auch an meiner Anspruchshaltung nicht spurlos vorbei: Es werden dem Erwerber heute Farb- und Materialwelten maßgeschneidert zu jedem Objekt vorgeschlagen, die im Einklang mit der Architektur stehen. Das war und ist für mich einschneidend und geschmacksbildend gewesen. In meiner ersten Immobilie hätte ich wohl niemals alle Wände grau gestrichen – im jetzigen Zuhause haben wir alle Schattierungen von Grau gewählt. Der SCHMITZ-Box sei Dank!

*In der RALF-SCHMITZ-Box befinden sich der Grundriss sowie Muster der möglichen Material- und Farbwelten für das Interieur der erworbenen Immobilie ...*

DR. JOCHEN BEST: ... ich würde diese Box sogar einen Fan-Artikel nennen! Wenn es in der Besprechung um die Ausstattung geht, dann bekommt man diese wunderschöne, in Leinen gehüllte Box, die es sehr erleichtert, das richtige Mobiliar auszusuchen und zusammen mit den Mustern ein Moodboard für sich zu erstellen. Ich habe die Box bereits an Freunde als Inspiration verliehen. Eine tolle Idee!

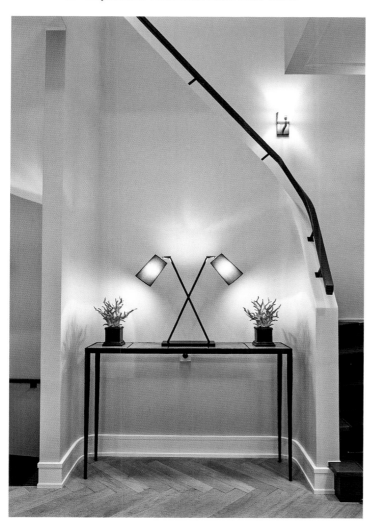

*Treppenaufgang in der zweigeschossigen Stadtvilla, die Teil des Ensembles Kentenich Hof ist —— Staircase in the two-storey urban villa, part of our Kentenich Hof ensemble*

*Herr Schmitz, wie entstand dieses smarte Tool?*

RICHARD ALEXANDER SCHMITZ: Zwischen Erwerb und Einzug liegt oft längere Zeit. Wir wollten den Kunden etwas Greifbares mitgeben, das Lust auf die Immobilie macht und mit dem sie das Interior-Design selbst festlegen können. Guter Nebeneffekt ist, dass Kunden sich früher mit der Ausstattung beschäftigen und uns ihre Entscheidungen mitteilen, die dann nicht in letzter Minute ausgeführt werden müssen.

*Herr Dr. Best, kann uns gute Architektur wie die von RALF SCHMITZ zu glücklicheren Menschen machen?*

DR. JOCHEN BEST: Sicherlich fühle ich mich in schöner Architektur wohler und gehe dadurch freundlicher mit meiner Umwelt um. Ich tanke in meinem stilvollen Zuhause Kraft, lebe so, wie ich es mir vorstelle und bin zufrieden. Insofern: Ja, gute Architektur macht glücklich!

---

*When you enter a RALF SCHMITZ building, you enter a world with a particular architectural and aesthetic identity. Dr Best, you've been a fan of this world for over 25 years – could you tell us why?*

DR JOCHEN BEST: It's something I feel as soon as I walk into the large lobby of a SCHMITZ building. There I'm greeted by elegant lamps and high-quality wooden doors, a polished brass bell plate, and tasteful furniture such as a handsome console table, with fine art hung above it – for me, these are typical SCHMITZ characteristics. Understated chic without brash accessories or architectural extravagances that quickly date – that's something you rarely see done so impeccably.

*Do you still remember what earlier RALF SCHMITZ properties looked like?*

DR JOCHEN BEST: Yes, it was way back in the mid 1980s: I was a medical student at the time so couldn't afford a RALF SCHMITZ apartment, but I was a keen follower of the firm's work and took an interest in the properties' floor plans and fittings. It was a kind of hobby of mine to visit all the Düsseldorf show homes. They were really beautiful even then, but overall the feel was a little more sober and the style not quite as impeccable as it is today. The company was already installing spacious bathrooms, using fabulous ceramics and elegant parquet flooring – not with the same incredible attention to detail as today but already of unbeatable quality nonetheless. I think you could already see the beginnings of the style it has since perfected; all the same, the properties RALF SCHMITZ is developing today never cease to impress and amaze me.

*Herr Schmitz, your family-run firm is now in the hands of the fourth and fifth generations. At what age did your love of architecture first manifest itself?*

RICHARD ALEXANDER SCHMITZ: Given that it was and is always present around the dinner table, like a member of the family so to speak, the firm does play a very big part. Even as a child, I came into contact with architecture every day. My parents are true aesthetes! Quality and longevity have always been very important to them, so, when we were kids, their philosophy was ever-present. On weekend outings and family holidays in my childhood, my parents would stop in front of interesting buildings and there'd be a little lesson on the style of architecture each time. That always really tickled me, although it was only when I got older that I genuinely found it interesting. My parents would photograph things that caught their attention, especially beautiful doors and other such details. The photographs would then go into the company archives and resurface during a particular development.

*Sonderwünsche erwünscht: Für alle nötigen Vorrichtungen beim Einbau einer Biosauna sorgte das SCHMITZ-Team —— Special requests welcome: the SCHMITZ team organised all necessary fittings for the installation of a bio sauna*

## "THEY SUGGEST BESPOKE COLOUR AND MATERIAL SCHEMES THAT BLEND PERFECTLY WITH THE PROPERTY'S ARCHITECTURE."

*Dr Best, does it inspire greater confidence to buy property from a traditional firm?*

DR JOCHEN BEST: Alongside the exceptional build quality, the fact that RALF SCHMITZ is a family business is definitely also an important factor. I come from such a family myself and, naturally, I'm happy to be able to support such businesses as a loyal customer. Also, you're always dealing with the same people, which is very reassuring when buying a property – knowing who is in charge and who is responsible gives you security, confidence and a feeling of loyalty, especially when you're investing your own money. No one wants to be left with a half-finished property whose developer has disappeared into the mist.

*A client base that includes multiple generations of the same family is no doubt a source of pride. What kind of challenges does that pose for the firm today in terms of maintaining those very high standards?*

RICHARD ALEXANDER SCHMITZ: Obviously we're very happy to have built up such an excellent reputation – but the credit for that goes to my forebears. For my generation, it comes with a great sense of responsibility and that needs to be handled carefully. Maintaining those high standards is a basic principle: we do our best every day and aim to keep on improving. That's a precept we all adhere to.

*Classical yet contemporary architectural forms, elegant colour schemes, exquisite materials: when you buy a RALF SCHMITZ home – in your case, for the third time – do your own standards rise? Does it influence your personal style?*

DR JOCHEN BEST: Definitely. You can clearly trace how the firm has perfected its style over the past five years, creating architecture in which many aspects have been continually refined. I've lived in three very different RALF SCHMITZ properties and have witnessed and experienced these changes at first hand. They were already homes of a high quality, now they are homes of the highest quality. My own attitudes have not been immune to that progression. When you buy a RALF SCHMITZ property today, they suggest bespoke colour and material schemes that blend perfectly with its architecture.

*Die Oberfläche der maßangefertigten Küche heißt Softtouch und passt perfekt zur samtigen Materialwelt des angrenzenden Bereichs* —— *The finish of the custom-made kitchen goes by the name Softtouch and blends perfectly with the velvety material mix in the adjacent living area*

That has had a big impact and helped to shape my tastes. At my first property, I would never have painted the walls grey, but for my current home, we chose a whole range of greys – thanks to the SCHMITZ Box!!

*The SCHMITZ Box contains the purchased property's floor plan plus material and colour swatches for possible interior schemes...*
DR JOCHEN BEST: I'm a big fan of this box. When it comes to talking about the interior fittings during consultations, you get given a beautiful linen-clad box that makes it so much easier to choose the right furnishings and, with its samples, allows you to put together a kind of personal mood board. I've even lent mine to friends as a source of inspiration. Such a great idea!

> "THE PROPERTIES RALF SCHMITZ
> IS DEVELOPING TODAY
> NEVER CEASE TO IMPRESS
> AND AMAZE ME."

*Herr Schmitz, how did this clever little tool come about? How does it help your clients?*
RICHARD ALEXANDER SCHMITZ: Clients often have to wait a longish time between buying a property and moving in, so we came up with the idea of giving them something tangible that would whet their appetite for the fantastic home that awaits them – and allow them to start making decisions on the interior design. It also has the positive side-effect that clients start thinking about fixtures and fittings and letting us know their choices early on, meaning we don't have to act upon decisions at the last minute.

*Dr Best, can good architecture such as that created by RALF SCHMITZ make us happier individuals?*
DR JOCHEN BEST: I definitely feel more at ease being surrounded by attractive architecture and am friendlier to those around me as a result. My stylish home allows me to recharge my batteries, live how I want to live and feel content. So, yes, good architecture can bring happiness!

# STYLE SHOW: INTERIOR DESIGNS

OB *DEZENTES DEKOR* ODER *FANTASTISCHES FARBGEWITTER*: DIE GROSSZÜGIGEN GRUNDRISSE ERMÖGLICHEN ELEGANTE *WOHN-COUTURE*

FROM *ELEGANT RESTRAINT* TO EXPLOSIONS OF COLOUR – GENEROUS FLOOR PLANS ALLOW FOR *INDIVIDUALLY TAILORED* DECOR

FOTOS **TODD EBERLE, ANDREAS GEHRKE, GREGOR HOHENBERG** TEXT **BETTINA SCHNEUER**

*Raffinesse für die Ruhe: Im Schlafzimmer des Stadthauses in Berlin-Grunewald schmiegt sich das komfortable Boxspringbett mit bezogenem Headboard in eine passgenaue Wandnische*

*Restful refinement: the comfortable box-spring bed's upholstered headboard sits neatly within the bedroom alcove at a Grunewald townhouse*

STADTHAUS

*Griegstraße, Berlin*

Auch den eleganten Wohnsalon kreierte das
Studio Oliver Jungel. Der Bronzekamin ist ein
Unikat, die „Infante"-Sessel stammen von
Liaigre, das Sofa wurde extra auf Maß gefertigt

Designed by Studio Oliver Jungel, this elegant
living room has a one-of-a-kind bronze fireplace
and "Infante" chairs by Liaigre; the sofa is bespoke

111

# STADTHAUS

*Griegstraße, Berlin*

*Bodentiefe Fenster lassen Licht in die großzügige Premiumküche mit Kochinsel strömen, wo Pietra Grigia Stilakzente setzt*

*Floor-to-ceiling windows allow light to flood into the spacious high-end kitchen, which boasts an island unit and Pietra Grigia accents*

*Hanseatische Oberklasse: In Othmarschen
prunkt auf kerngeräuchtertem Eichenparkett
ein glamouröser Vintage-Esstisch aus den
Forties von dem US-Designer Paul T. Frankl*

*A vintage 1940s table by US designer Paul
T. Frankl forms the glamorous centrepiece
of this show home's dining room, which
has parquet flooring in core-smoked oak*

# HAUS BAHREN

*Roosens Weg, Hamburg*

Dezente Noblesse durch wertige Materialien
und Möbel-Mix im Wohnzimmer: Unter der
Wandleuchte „265" von Flos stehen ein
Sofaunikat und Vintagesessel von Liaigre

Quality materials and carefully mixed furniture
add up to a look of understated elegance,
with a SCHMITZ sofa and two vintage Liaigre
chairs arranged beneath a Flos "265" lamp

*Klassikertrio als Deckenpendel: Die „A330S"
von Artek erhellt sanft den erlesenen Essbereich.
Ovaler Esstisch „Kops": Van Rossum*

*A refined oval dining table ("Kops" by
Van Rossum) is bathed in soft light by a trio of
Artek's classic "A330S" pendant lamps*

# HAUS FRIEDRICH

## *Goldfinkweg, Berlin*

*Kluge Kombination: Neben dem Masterbedroom
liegt die ausgefeilt gebaute Ankleide aus
grau gebeizter Eiche mit praktischer Sitzbank*

*Smartly done: the dressing room next to the
master bedroom combines fitted cabinetry in grey-
stained oak with a built-in window seat*

*Wohnbühne, farbenfreudig gestaltet vom Stilmagazin Architectural Digest: Unter dem Lüster „Modo" von Roll & Hill rahmen auf einem Perroquet-Teppich (Galerie Diurne) „Sant'Ambrogio"-Sofas von Azucena den Espasso-Couchtisch*

*Azucena "Sant'Ambrogio" sofas flank an Espasso coffee table in a colour-filled living room decorated by design magazine Architectural Digest Germany. "Perroquet" rug from Galerie Diurne; "Modo" chandelier by Roll & Hill*

# HAUS WEYHE
## Peter-Lenné-Straße, Berlin

*Ganz links: himmelblauer Küchenkosmos. Der Tisch mit Bronzefuß wurde im Atelier Stefan Leo gefertigt, daran französische Vintage-Stühle. Luxusherd: „CornuFé 90". Daneben: Bibliothek mit Kamin, maßgefertigten Regalen und Lesesesseln von Amy Somerville*

*Far left: pride of place in the pale blue kitchen goes to a high-end CornuFé 90 cooker; the bronze-legged table is by Atelier Stefan Leo, around it are vintage French chairs. Left: library with custom-made shelving plus fireside reading chairs by Amy Somerville*

*Im Grunewalder Stadtvillen-Duo kleidet Marmor das En-Suite-Masterbad. Das Bett „Frou Frou" mit kapitoniertem Kopfteil stammt von Promemoria*

*At this Grunewald show apartment, the master bedroom boasts a marble-clad en-suite bath plus Promemoria's "Frou Frou" button-headboard bed*

# HUBERTUSGÄRTEN

## *Hubertusbader Straße, Berlin*

*Die klassizierende Symmetrie der Architektur setzt sich innen kongenial fort: Edles dunkles Holz und feiner Stuck adeln den lichten Wohnraum*

*The exterior's classical symmetry is echoed by the living room, in which dark wood and first-class plasterwork make for a refined look*

Die Show-Apartments von RALF SCHMITZ feiern fabelhafte Stilpartys: Gestaltet von renommierten Designern im Auftrag des Traditionsunternehmens, sollen diese Wohnungen erlebbar machen, wie das eigene Zuhause in diesen exklusiven Domizilen aussehen könnte, und Potenziale aufzeigen. Sie sollen Käufer, die sich hier umsehen, inspirieren zu einem gelungenen Interieur, das ihrem individuellen Lebensgefühl entspricht. Und sie stellen klar: Die herausragende Formensprache im Äußeren findet ihre Pendants in prägnanten Innenarchitekturen.

Die Einrichtungen überzeugen, weil sie – trotz ihrer immensen Vielfalt – allesamt eines gemeinsam haben: Sie besitzen über gegenwärtige Trends hinaus Bestand und bieten umfassenden Komfort. So arrangierte Oliver Jungel, international arbeitender Designspezialist mit Sitz in Düsseldorf, dort eine spektakuläre Schauraumwohnung im Haus Hardenberg in Düsseltal. Seine typische, auf die Essenz reduzierte Eleganz kommt auch bei einem neuen Bauvorhaben in der Linienstraße in Berlin-Mitte zum Tragen.

*Architectural Digest*, das führende deutsche Magazin in Sachen Style, tauchte ein großzügiges Hauptstadt-Hochparterre in Juwelen- und Gewürzfarben und verwandelte es in eine flamboyante Wunderkammer voll mit ikonischen *pieces*. Und beim Kurfürstendamm stattete 2016 Tomas Maier, Creative Director von Bottega Veneta, im Wohnpalais Eisenzahn 1 eine Musterwohnung mit jenen üppigen Sofas und mit Flechtleder veredelten Stücken aus, für welche die hochklassige Home Collection des berühmten italienischen Luxuslabels gefeiert wird.

Zum mühelosen Spagat zwischen High End auf der einen Seite und Heimeligkeit auf der anderen tragen natürlich die ausgefeilten Grundrisse ebenso bei wie die repräsentativen Ausstattungen aller Wohnungen: etwa hochwertige Badarmaturen und -objekte, erlesene Bodenbeläge aus Naturstein und Holz oder noble Kamine; dazu hohe Decken, die an Altbau-Etagen erinnern, und klassische Stuckleisten – gepaart mit technischen Raffinessen wie etwa Klimadecken, separat steuerbaren Rollläden oder Bussystemen. Luxus definiert sich hier auch als Sorgenfreiheit und besonderer Lebenskomfort.

Für die eingangs erwähnte Stilparty gibt es übrigens die ideale Gastgeberin. Sie heißt Grau und ist die stille Königin der neutralen Farben – zeitlos, edel und zudem äußerst tolerant. Denn fast keine Farbe lässt andere Töne und Materialien, ob diese nun zart oder kräftig sind, neben sich so fabelhaft zur Geltung kommen wie Grau. Und keine andere Farbe entspricht dem Zeitgeist besser, weil sie ebenso facettenreich ist wie dieser. Grau kann zugleich urban, natürlich oder klassisch wirken und entsprechend kombiniert werden. Insofern passt diese stille Königin eben auch perfekt zu jedem RALF-SCHMITZ-Zuhause.

---

RALF SCHMITZ show apartments are sumptuous celebrations of style. Created by renowned designers, they aim to showcase decorative possibilities and illustrate what a home in a particular development might look like. They also act as a source of inspiration, helping buyers to put together stylish interiors that chime with how they want to live. And they demonstrate that a RALF SCHMITZ building is as thoughtfully designed on the inside as it is on the outside.

Despite their diverse decors, these compelling show homes all have one thing in common: they combine luxurious living with an enduring style that looks beyond short-lived trends. For one show apartment in Berlin, Düsseldorf-based designer Oliver Jungel created spectacular interiors based on the very best of what Italian furniture maker Promemoria has to offer, while his trademark pared-down elegance can soon also be admired at Linienstrasse, an upcoming Berlin project. Leading style magazine *Architectural Digest* Germany brought spice and gemstone hues to a spacious apartment in the capital, transforming it into a flamboyant showcase full of iconic designs. And, in 2016, Tomas Maier, creative director at Italian luxury label Bottega Veneta, created a show home for the exclusive Eisenzahn 1 development featuring the generously proportioned sofas and woven leather accents for which the label's superb Home Collection is renowned.

In each of these spaces, high-end design elements blend effortlessly with a homely ambience, thanks to the apartments' carefully thought-out floor plans and to first-class fixtures and fittings such as quality bathroom furniture and taps, cosy fireplaces and floors of fine wood and natural stone – paired with high-tech refinements such as climate control ceilings, individually operable blinds and electronic control systems: Luxury defined as comfortable, hassle-free living.

For the aforementioned celebrations, there could be no better host than grey, the quiet queen of neutral shades. Timeless and elegant, grey is uniquely adept at making other materials and soft or bold shades look great. It's also supremely versatile and thus very contemporary, it can be urban, natural or traditional – perfect for a SCHMITZ home.

*Unangestrengt reinterpretierte Tradition
großbürgerlicher Grundrisse mit modernem
Flair: das luxuriös-komfortable Living*

*Modern furnishings and a contemporary
take on grand 19th-century floor plans create
an effortlessly luxurious living room*

# HAUS HARDENBERG
## *Tiergartenstraße, Düsseldorf*

*Diskretes Farbspektrum: Rauch, Silber,
Zink und Anthrazit prägen das
Dining im klassischen Zooviertel-Solitär*

*Muted shades of smoke, silver, zinc
and anthracite define the dining room
of this Zooviertel apartment*

*Im eleganten Wohnpalais beim
Kurfürstendamm kocht eine Eigentümerin
in ihrer coolen Küche von Bulthaup*

*An owner's sleek Bulthaup kitchen at
RALF SCHMITZ's prestigious development
just off Kurfürstendamm*

# EISENZAHN 1

*Eisenzahnstraße, Berlin*

# REPORT: TRADITIONAL ARCHITECTURAL PRINCIPLES

Mit *zeitloser Ästhetik* trägt RALF SCHMITZ
die Eleganz klassischer Architektur in die Zukunft

With its attention to *timeless aesthetics*, RALF SCHMITZ
transports the elegance of classic architecture into the future

ILLUSTRATIONEN **SEBASTIAN TREESE ARCHITEKTEN**    TEXT **HOLGER REINERS**

Schönheit und Eleganz: Diese Begriffe sorgen seit Jahren für heftige Diskussionen unter Architekten. Darf man denn heute noch so bauen wie im Stil von vor über 100 Jahren, ist das nicht ein Verrat an der Moralität des Berufsstandes? Würde uns nicht so eine scheinbar heile Welt angeboten, wird Architektur nicht so zum Seelentröster in einem rauen Alltag, obwohl sie doch besser andere Prioritäten setzen sollte? Hardliner unter den heutigen Architekten kämpfen verbissen um die sogenannte Moderne mit ihren Stereotypen und um ihr Entwurfsprinzip des rechten Winkels als Maß aller Dinge.

RALF SCHMITZ hat sich jedoch nie um irgendeinen oktroyierten Mainstream gekümmert. Als Auftraggeber renommierter Entwurfsbüros ist das Unternehmen stets konsequent seiner ganz eigenen Sicht auf Architektur gefolgt: einer Architektur der Eleganz und des Wohlbefindens. Nennen wir es doch – ebenso einfach wie kompliziert – so: Es soll Schönheit entstehen. Dies umzusetzen ist eine Gratwanderung, denn das Staunen über das Phänomen Schönheit und die Versuche, Schönheit zu definieren, zählen seit der Antike, seit Platons Satz, dass das Schöne der Glanz des Wahren sei (*pulchrum est splendor veri*), zu den wichtigsten Themen der Philosophie. Schönheit kommt mithin vom Scheinen – nicht im Sinne einer bloßen Vorspiegelung, sondern vom Leuchten, vom Glänzen. Der Glanz der Wahrheit, der Wirklichkeit ist also das Schöne.

Und dies kann eigentlich jeder erkennen. Denn die biologische Forschung hat ergeben, dass wir alle eine Art Kunst- und Symmetrie-Gen in uns tragen, dass wir alle also jene Parameter der Schönheit wahrnehmen, die seit Platon nichts an Gültigkeit eingebüßt haben. Was ist die Fassade eines Hauses anderes als ein Gesicht – das ist ja der Ursprung des Wortes Fassade. Ein schönes Gesicht, eine einladende Fassade heben unsere Stimmung, sie sind für uns ein Wahrnehmungsbalsam. Alle Gegenbewegungen der Architektur scheiterten mit kurzem Verfallsdatum – jedoch belästigen ihre gebauten Ergebnisse unsere ästhetische Wahrnehmung noch über Jahrzehnte hinaus, wie leider jeder Spaziergang durch eine beliebige Metropole zeigt.

Das Unternehmen RALF SCHMITZ schafft dagegen architektonische Adressen, die nicht nur jeden Bewohner auch ästhetisch glücklich machen, sondern jedem Menschen im öffentlichen Raum visuell zugänglich sind und mit staunender Freude wahrgenommen werden: ein unterschwelliger, freudiger Impuls am Weg. Dies gelingt, weil für die Projektentwürfe in Kempen, Düsseldorf, Berlin und Hamburg, also am

Stammsitz und an nunmehr drei Niederlassungen des Unternehmens, nur sorgfältig ausgewählte und sehr renommierte Büros beauftragt werden: Besonders zu nennen sind hier RKW Architektur +, Petra und Paul Kahlfeldt Architekten, Sebastian Treese Architekten sowie Hilmer Sattler Architekten Ahlers Albrecht. Deren Vorstellungen harmonieren aufs Beste mit den hohen Ansprüchen des Traditionsunternehmens, dessen baukulturelle Wurzeln bis ins Jahr 1864 zurückreichen.

## ARCHITEKTONISCH REIZVOLLE, BESONDERE BAUWERKE, DIE IHRE UMGEBUNG ADELN.

Die Stadtvillen und Stadthäuser von RALF SCHMITZ stellen sich in ihrer stolzen und doch zurückhaltenden Würde sowohl dem Betrachter als vor allem auch dem Bewohner als die Botschafter eines eleganten Zuhauses dar. Für den Käufer eines solchen Domizils wird es das Passepartout für die eigene Lebenswelt. Erlesene Materialien, gekonnte Verarbeitung und raffinierte Einbauten, überhaupt die außerordentliche Detaillierung des Gebauten im Äußeren wie im Inneren als Gesamtkunstwerk, dienen als reizvolle, zu bespielende Grundlage einer persönlichen Möblierung durch den neuen Eigentümer.

Jede Wohnung, jedes Stadthaus gewährleistet zudem durch kluge Grundrisse kostbare Privatsphäre. Das ist die große Kunst der Bauwerke aus dem Hause RALF SCHMITZ: Alle Projekte, stets geprägt von der allgegenwärtigen Liebe zur Architektur, bieten ein elegantes Ambiente als Fond für eigene Wohnvorstellungen von Privatheit und Repräsentation. Und zugleich bilden sie in den Straßen und an den Plätzen, an denen sie entstehen, reizvolle architektonische Besonderheiten, weil sie einer zeitlosen Formensprache huldigen. Schönheit ist eben noch immer der Glanz der Wahrheit.

---

Beauty and elegance. These concepts have been much debated in architecture over the years. Is it appropriate to build today in a style from one hundred years ago? Is that not moral treason against the profession? Wouldn't that be an illusion of a seemingly perfect world? Would architecture morph into a mere soul-comforter in a harsh everyday life, although it should better set other priorities? Hardliners among today's architects brandish stereotypes in their bitter fight for so-called modernism, dying on the sword of the right angle as the end-all be-all of design.

RALF SCHMITZ, however, has never been interested in going along with an imposed-on mainstream. By hiring renowned architectural design firms, the company has always

PETRA UND PAUL KAHLFELDT
ARCHITEKTEN

———

*Leo-Blech-Platz, Berlin-Grunewald: 2 Stadtvillen*
*mit je 3 Wohnungen von 211 bis 308 qm*

RKW ARCHITEKTUR +
RHODE KELLERMANN WAWROWSKY

———

*Deger's, Düsseldorf-Flingern: 11 Wohnungen, darunter*
*2 Maisonette-Townhouses mit Privatgärten, von 139 bis 245 qm*

SEBASTIAN TREESE ARCHITEKTEN

*Greifweg, Düsseldorf-Oberkassel: 3 Stadtvillen mit insgesamt 14 Wohnungen
von 114 bis 204 qm sowie 2 Penthouses mit 175 und 181 qm*

been true to its own vision of architecture: one of elegance and well-being. The mandate is as simple as it is complex – to create beauty – and to achieve it is to walk a fine line; since antiquity, philosophy has grappled with the awe of the phenomenon of beauty while attempting to define it. Pulchrum est splendour veri, wrote Plato: beauty is the splendour of truth. The shine of truth, of reality, is beauty. And this, in fact, can be recognised by all.

## ARCHITECTURALLY APPEALING, REMARKABLE BUILDINGS THAT ENNOBLE THEIR VICINITY.

Biological research has proven that we all carry in us a kind of gene for an appreciation of art and symmetry, that we inherently perceive the same parameters of beauty that Plato sought to explain. What difference, then, is there between the façade of a building and a face? Even their linguistic roots are the same. A beautiful face, an inviting façade, can lift our spirits, act as a kind of salve for the senses. All of architecture's countermovements have failed the test of time and yet what they have left behind still irritates our innate sense of aesthetics, and will irritate it for decades to come, as any stroll through any big city can attest.

RALF SCHMITZ, in contrast, creates unique architectural addresses that are not only aesthetically pleasing to their residents but also visually accessible to the public, who appreciate them with awe and joy: subliminal, friendly stimuli as we pass by. Selecting only the most renowned design firms for the projects in Kempen, Düsseldorf, Berlin and Hamburg, home now to the company's four offices, has been crucial to this success.

Of particular note are RKW Architektur +, Petra und Paul Kahlfeldt Architekten, Sebastian Treese Architekten and Hilmer Sattler Architekten Ahlers Albrecht. Their visions harmonise perfectly with the high standards of the long-standing firm whose history of building culture is rooted in the mid-nineteenth century.

HILMER SATTLER ARCHITEKTEN AHLERS ALBRECHT

*Achenbachstraße, Düsseldorf-Düsseltal: 12 Wohnungen von
158 bis 198 qm sowie 1 Penthouse mit 220 qm*

PETRA UND PAUL KAHLFELDT ARCHITEKTEN

*Haus Bahren, Hamburg-Othmarschen: 5 Wohnungen,*
*darunter 1 Penthouse, von 135 bis 258 qm*

SEBASTIAN TREESE ARCHITEKTEN

*Linienstraße, Berlin-Mitte: 7 Wohnungen,*
*darunter 1 Penthouse, von 93 bis 212 qm*

With their proud and yet reserved dignity, the urban villas and residential buildings by RALF SCHMITZ are ambassadors of elegant living both to passers-by and, above all, to their residents.

For homebuyers, it becomes the framework of their environment. Exquisite materials, skilled workmanship, refined built-ins, the fine physical details both outside and in come together as a total work of art and serve as an inspiring foundation on which each owner can build her personal space. With their smart floor plans, each apartment, each home provides precious private spaces. That is the great achievement of RALF SCHMITZ's architecture: all of the projects, consistently shaped by the pervasive love of architecture, offer an elegant ambience as the basis of one's own personal preferences for privacy and representation. And at the same time, they are immensely attractive architectural additions to the streets and squares where they stand because they pay homage to a classical aesthetic language that stands and will stand the test of time.

Beauty is indeed still the splendour of truth.

RKW ARCHITEKTUR + RHODE KELLERMANN WAWROWSKY

*Kentenich Hof, Düsseldorf-Golzheim: Haupthaus mit 20 Wohnungen, dahinter*
*2 frei stehende Stadthäuser, von 110 bis 300 qm*

# AT A GLANCE: FIREPLACES

ES GIBT NUR WENIG SCHÖNERES, ALS ZU HAUSE
GEMÜTLICH EIN KNISTERNDES FEUER IM KAMIN ZU ENTZÜNDEN.
EINE STILSCHAU FLAMBOYANTER FEUERSTÄTTEN

THERE ARE FEW THINGS MORE COMFORTING THAN
THE WARM GLOW OF A REAL FIRE.
WE PRESENT A FEW OF OUR FAVOURITE SURROUNDS

BERLIN, HUBERTUSGÄRTEN

*Kontrastreich: Die lichte Maske aus „Mocca Creme"-Kalkstein ergänzt ein Passepartout aus edlem polierten Nero Assoluto (2010)*

*A pale Mocca Creme limestone surround contrasts with a sleek fascia of polished Nero Assoluto (2010)*

BERLIN, EISENZAHN I

*Monochromes Meisterstück: Maske aus italienischem Limestone Persiano und Vorgelege aus schwarzem Metall (2016)*

*Masterpiece in monochrome: Italian Persiano limestone surround meets black metal hearth (2016)*

BERLIN, NIKISCHSTRASSE

*Im Denkmal „Landhaus Pinn", erbaut 1923, wurde auch der historische Kamin in der Halle sensibel aufgearbeitet (2012)*

*At Landhaus Pinn, a historic villa from 1923, even the period hallway fireplace has been sensitively restored (2012)*

BERLIN, HAUS WEYHE

*Rasant: New Port Saint Laurent, ein dunkler Marmor aus Marokko mit goldener Äderung, rahmt die Feuerstelle (2013)*

*New Port Saint Laurent, a gold-veined dark marble from Morocco, creates a strikingly framed open fire (2013)*

HAMBURG, HAUS BAHREN

*Hingucker: Eine besonders breite, profilierte*
*Kaminmaske aus auffälligem Port-*
*Black-Marmor mit rasanter Äderung (2014)*

*An extra-wide format and strikingly veined*
*Port Black marble make this moulded*
*surround a particular eye-catcher (2014)*

DÜSSELDORF, HAUS HARDENBERG

*Helle Freude: Vor dem geschlossenen Kamin*
*mit portugiesischer Kalksteinmaske muss*
*das Parkett nicht abgedeckt werden (2008)*

*The closed glass front of this Portuguese*
*limestone fireplace meant no hearth plate was*
*needed for the parquet floor (2008)*

DÜSSELDORF, TIERGARTENSTRASSE

*Souverän mondän: Ein Bodenfries aus*
*Carrara-Marmor vollzieht die kantige Form*
*der Grigio-Carnico-Maske nach (2008)*

*Refined lines: a floor frieze of Carrara*
*marble echoes the angular*
*Grigio Carnico surround (2008)*

KEMPEN, GRACHTENPARK

*Licht-Spiele hinter Glas: geschlossener*
*Kamin in dem Ensemble aus Einzel-, Reihen-*
*und Mehrfamilienhäusern (2013)*

*Flames behind glass: an example*
*from a mixed development of houses and*
*apartment blocks (2013)*

127

# THE BEAUTY OF ARCHITECTURAL MODELS

MASSSTABS- UND DETAILGETREUE *MINIATUREN*
ÜBERSETZEN DIGITALE PLÄNE IN PLASTISCHE
FORMEN: DAS *KÜNFTIGE ZUHAUSE* ALS 3-D-UNIKAT

ACCURATE AND TO SCALE, THESE
UNIQUE *MINIATURES* TRANSFORM DIGITAL PLANS
INTO THREE-DIMENSIONAL REALITY

FOTOS **GREGOR HOHENBERG, RALPH RICHTER** TEXT **BETTINA SCHNEUER**

*Die Stadtvilla auf dem Eck-Ensemble
Dahlem Duo im Maßstab 1:50 entstand
bei Monath + Menzel aus hellem Ahorn.
Zu sehen ist der separate Zugang zum
Hochparterre der Triplex-Wohnung,
darüber liegt der Balkon des Masterbades*

*1:50 scale, light-maple model of the villa
from the Dahlem Duo corner ensemble. Built
by Monath + Menzel, it shows the triplex's
separate ground floor entrance, above which
is the master bathroom's balcony*

Zur Gelfertstraße liegen die beiden
Stadthäuser mit realen Wohnnutzflächen von
über 400 qm. Die Geschosshöhen von bis
zu 3,50 m schrumpfen im Modell auf 7 cm

Offering over 400 sqm of living space, these two
urban villas on Gelfertstrasse boast
ceiling heights of up to 3.50 m – which shrink
to just 7 cm in the model version

Um den Ton der Ziegelfassade
von Haus Weyhe anzudeuten, wurde
rötliches Kirschholz verwendet

Reddish cherrywood was used to denote
the brickwork of Haus Weyhe's façade

*Für die große Fassadenansicht des Wohnpalais Eisenzahn 1 brauchte es gut zwei Monate. Auf eine MDF-Tragestruktur wurde Ahorn aufgebracht: als Furnier für flache Bereiche und als Vollholz für die Gesimse und Erker, deren perfekt vom Plan übertragenen Schwünge die hohe Schule des Modellbaus bedeuten*

---

*This large front-elevation model of our stately Eisenzahn 1 development took some two months to create. It comprises an MDF support structure plus maple veneer for flat surfaces and solid maple for cornices and bays, the latter's perfectly rendered curves marking the apogee of model-making precision*

*Die Düsseldorfer Modellbauer Einhaus schufen aus weiß lackiertem Polystyrol das Projekt Hubertusgärten, Berlin-Grunewald*

*Einhaus of Düsseldorf created this white polystyrene model of the Hubertusgärten ensemble in Berlin's Grunewald district*

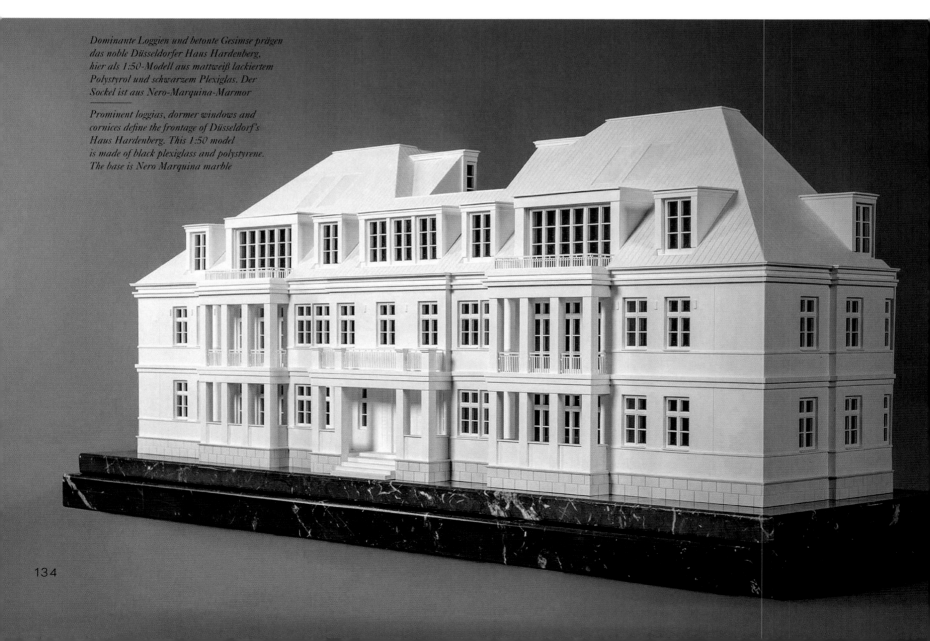

*Dominante Loggien und betonte Gesimse prägen das noble Düsseldorfer Haus Hardenberg, hier als 1:50-Modell aus mattweiß lackiertem Polystyrol und schwarzem Plexiglas. Der Sockel ist aus Nero-Marquina-Marmor*

*Prominent loggias, dormer windows and cornices define the frontage of Düsseldorf's Haus Hardenberg. This 1:50 model is made of black plexiglass and polystyrene. The base is Nero Marquina marble*

Ein wenig nach Vanille und nach Harz duftet es hier, aromatisch und ledrig. Dieser Raum in der Berliner Manufaktur Monath + Menzel ist das Herz des Holzmodellbaus, dort lagern Ahorn, fast ohne Maserung und wunderbar hell, und Birnbaum, ein wenig dunkler und auch gleichmäßig gewachsen. Dazu seltener eingesetzte Hölzer wie rötliche Kirsche, dunkles Teak oder die „Schöne Else", eine dezent gezeichnete Wildobstart. Eiche hat eine dominante Maserung und wird eher in weniger detaillierten Modellen verbaut.

Aus Ahorn sind deswegen die meisten der Architekturmodelle, die für RALF SCHMITZ bei Monath + Menzel angefertigt wurden: Das Ensemble Dahlem Duo etwa, für das man auch wegen der aufwendig in 3-D gefrästen Geländemodulation über drei Monate brauchte, oder der Fassadenausschnitt des weißen Wohnpalais Eisenzahn 1 aus über tausend Einzelteilen, darunter die vielen Geländer, der Vorgartenzaun und das prächtige Portal aus geschwärzter Bronze. Für die dunkleren Backsteinfronten von Haus Weyhe dagegen kam ausnahmsweise Kirschholz zum Einsatz, für feine Details wie Stuckgesimse, Säulen oder Fensterläden und das Dach wiederum Ahorn. „Bits und Bytes, also ein am Computer entworfenes Gebilde, erhalten durch unser maßstabsgetreues Modell den Bezug zur Wirklichkeit", sagt Axel Monath, selbst Architekt, der 1985 mit zwei Partnern das Atelier gründete. „Filtern und kondensieren" müsse der Modellbauer und „aus den digitalen Daten die originäre Idee herausarbeiten" – „ein schmaler Grat zwischen zu wenigen oder zu vielen Details".

Grundrisse, Schnitte und Ansichten übersetzt sein Team in eine plastische Form. Seit der Frührenaissance setzen Bauherren und Architekten auf den Modellbau. Der geschieht heutzutage einerseits hochmodern: „Im steten Kontakt mit dem Architekten über Screenshots, Datentransfer und Skype-Konferenzen wird das Modell verfeinert." Und andererseits noch immer ganz altmodisch, per Hand als Unikat zusammengesetzt. Die Ergebnisse sind „einfach fantastisch", findet der Architekt Sebastian Treese, der sehr viel für RALF SCHMITZ arbeitet. „Ein solches Modell hat zwar keinen hohen intellektuellen Wert, aber sein Bau ist natürlich ein kleiner Testlauf, ob der Entwurf funktioniert."

Das Haus *en miniature* ist also ein autonomes Objekt: Es hält, schon wegen seiner unterschiedlicher Materialität und der Detailreduktion, eine ästhetische Distanz zu dem später real Gebauten – und bildet es dennoch erstmals dreidimensional ab. Seine kunstfertig entstandene Form beflügelt unsere Fantasie: So also soll unser neues Zuhause aussehen – wie wunderschön.

---

A hint of vanilla and resin hangs in the air – a leathery, aromatic scent – in this space at model makers Monath + Menzel. There are supplies of beautifully pale maple, almost devoid of grain, piles of pear wood, a little darker in hue but similarly even in its growth, as well as less frequently used varieties such as reddish cherrywood and dark teak. Oak, meanwhile, has too prominent a grain.

Most of the architectural models this large Berlin practice produces for RALF SCHMITZ are intricately assembled from maple. The Dahlem Duo ensemble took over three months to model, partly because the varied external topography necessitated complex 3D milling. Over a thousand individual pieces were required to make a section of the firm's prestigious Eisenzahn 1 development, with its many balconette railings, perimeter fence and imposing blackened bronze entrance. Cherrywood was chosen for the darker brick façades of Haus Weyhe, with maple used only for fine details such as plaster cornices, columns and window shutters as well as for the roof.

"With our scale models, we are able to turn bits and bytes, like a computer-generated form, into something real," says Axel Monath, an architect himself, who founded the practice in 1985 with two partners. The model maker's job, he says, is to "filter and distill", to "pick out the essential idea from the digital data," a task in which there is "a fine line between too few and too many details." His team translates digital floor plans, sections and elevations into a three-dimensional form. Models are something builders and architects have been using since the early Renaissance and today's are still individually hand-assembled. Modern technology, though, also plays its part: "We liaise constantly with the architect via screenshots, data transfers and Skype conferences in order to fine-tune the model." The results are "just fantastic", says architect Sebastian Treese, who has worked on numerous RALF SCHMITZ projects. "Models like these may be of no great intellectual value, but their construction is, of course, a small-scale test run for the design – does it actually work?"

A miniature building of this kind is, then, a unique object in its own right. There is a clear aesthetic difference between it and the actual building but it lets us admire the latter in three dimensions for the first time and thus allows us to better imagine our new home: so this is where we are going to live – can't wait!

*Städtebauliche Herausforderung im Maßstab 1:100: Der Klosterhof, neuer Nukleus der Altstadt, reagiert mit Respekt auf Ortsspezifika wie die Paterskirche und das ehemalige Kloster daneben. Seit 2014 prägen die gekonnt verzahnten Baukörper für Gewerbe und Wohnen die Stadtmitte von Kempen. Modell aus lackiertem Polystyrol, gebaut von Einhaus*

*1:100 scale model of a major urban planning challenge: the Klosterhof development responds sensitively to local specifics such as the historic church and adjacent former monastery. Its cleverly integrated residential and retail spaces have formed the heart of old Kempen since 2014*

„Am Computer entworfene Gebilde erhalten durch maßstabsgetreue Modelle den Bezug zur Wirklichkeit"

"Scale models turn computer-generated forms into something real"

*Öffentlich gefördert: Rund 1.500
Mietwohnungen, darunter knapp 420
Einheiten für Senioren, plus Gewerbe und
Kulturstätten entstanden in nur vier
Jahren Bauzeit. 1973 war die Backstein-
siedlung Düsseldorf-Reisholz bezugsfertig*

*Comprising around 1,500 rental apartments,
including almost 420 for the elderly,
as well as commercial premises and cultural
venues, this publicly funded brick estate
in the Reisholz area of Düsseldorf was
completed in 1973 after just four years' work*

*Modell für das Hochhaus der Heinrich Schmitz
KG am Hofgarten in Düsseldorf, fertig-
gestellt 1971: Über sechs Etagen mit Büros
liegen 13 weitere mit Eigentumswohnungen,
den Pavillonanbau bezog die Firma selbst*

*Model of the 1971 tower block built by Heinrich
Schmitz KG opposite Düsseldorf's Hofgarten.
It featured six storeys of office space with 13
storeys of apartments above; the pavilion-style
annexe became the firm's own local base*

# REPORT: RALF SCHMITZ AND THE FINE ARTS

Überragende *Baukunst* wird durch *Kunstwerke* perfekt ergänzt.
Ausgewählte Arbeiten und der Anspruch dahinter

Perfect partners: a look at the firm's commitment to combining
architecture and art – and at *selected works* in situ

TEXT **INA MARIE KÜHNAST**

*Den Pariser Jardin du Luxembourg ziert Jean Terzieffs Statue „La Femme aux Pommes" (1937), die Replik den Düsseldorfer Sophienhof ——— Replica of a Jean Terzieff statue at our Sophienhof development; the original stands in central Paris*

E r selbst halte es ein wenig wie Voltaire, sagt Ralf Schmitz. Der französische Philosoph ließ einst über die Bewertung von Kunst verlauten: „Jede Art von Kunst ist gut, außer der, die langweilig ist." Was nicht bedeutet, dass Ralf Schmitz so einfach und schnell von einer künstlerischen Arbeit zu überzeugen ist. „Ich bin recht anspruchsvoll und wählerisch und wirklich kein spontaner Käufer. Pro Jahr wird vielleicht eine Arbeit erworben, manchmal aber auch keine. Mit dem Kunsterwerb ist es wie mit dem Kauf eines Hauses – es braucht seine Zeit. Zudem hat meine Frau Vetorecht. Wenn sie dagegen stimmt, wird nicht gekauft." Neben dem Bauen ist also auch die Kunst bei dem Kempener Familiensache.

Wie viel die schönen Künste dem Unternehmer bedeuten, zeigt sich in seinem Verständnis für die gelungene Symbiose aus Architektur und bildender Kunst. Er sammelt nicht nur für sich privat, sondern bedenkt mit seinen Neuerwerbungen auch die Räumlichkeiten der inzwischen vier Firmenstandorte Kempen, Düsseldorf, Berlin und Hamburg. Und außerdem die kurz vor der Vollendung stehenden Bauprojekte des Traditionsunternehmens RALF SCHMITZ: So kommt es nicht selten vor, dass man dort in Foyers, Treppenhäusern oder Gartenanlagen auf Fotografien, Gemälde oder Skulpturen trifft, die aus

*Am Düsseldorfer Hofgarten (1971): Hieronymus Schmitz (ganz links) neben dem Bildhauer Blasius Spreng, der den Springbrunnen aus Bronzequadern mit Messingkugel entworfen hatte* —— *Hofgarten, Düsseldorf: this fountain of bronze blocks and brass globe was a specially commissioned piece by the sculptor Blasius Spreng (1971)*

der familieneigenen Sammlung persönlich für das jeweilige neue Gebäude ausgewählt wurden. Diese Verbindung ist Ralf Schmitz wichtig: „Projekte wie Eisenzahn 1, deren Showrooms mit Werken aus unserer Sammlung dekoriert wurden, sind für mich wie Gesamtkunstwerke", sagt er. Bedauernd fügt er hinzu, dass es selten geworden sei, die einst enge Verbindung von Kunstwerk und Architektur aufrechtzuerhalten. „Heutzutage hat es sich durchgesetzt, dass Architekten kaum noch bildende Kunst in ihren Bauten haben wollen, weil sie sich selbst oft als Künstler verstehen – und ihre realisierten Entwürfe als das eigentliche Kunstwerk an sich."

An die erste Arbeit, die er sich kaufte, erinnert er sich noch gut. Sie war vom Düsseldorfer Maler Norbert Tadeusz und hieß „Calla". Farbenfroh und figurativ. Das Werk sei aber nicht ausschlaggebend gewesen für eine gewisse Richtung, die er bevorzuge. „In unserer Sammlung sind die unterschiedlichsten Stile und Richtungen vorhanden. Geschmack entwickelt und verändert sich ja über die Jahre. Mein frühes Interesse galt verstärkt figurativer Malerei, heute faszinieren mich auch abstrakte Arbeiten." Wollte man dennoch einen Sammlungsschwerpunkt ausmachen, dann wäre dies sicherlich „eine gewisse lokale Note": Werke des Lichtkünstlers Adolf Luther

und des ZERO-Vertreters Otto Piene, malerische Gegenstandswelten Dieter Kriegs, reliefartige Gemälde von Günther Uecker oder farbmonochrome Kissenbilder des Malers Gotthard Graubner sind zu finden – die meisten auf die eine oder andere Art mit dem Rheinland verbunden.

## „ES HAT SICH DURCHGESETZT, DASS ARCHITEKTEN KAUM NOCH KUNST IN IHREN BAUTEN HABEN WOLLEN."

Es wäre ein wenig überzogen, zu behaupten, der Sinn für die schönen Künste läge bei den Kempener Unternehmern seit Generationen in der Familie. Tatsächlich war Hieronymus Schmitz, SCHMITZ-Firmenchef in dritter Generation und Vater des jetzigen Geschäftsführers, der Erste, der sich neben der Architektur auch der Kunst verschrieben hatte. Er besaß zudem ein ausgeprägtes Verständnis für verschiedenste Kunstgattungen und gab dieses gern weiter: Hieronymus Schmitz hatte beim berühmten Hochschullehrer Heinrich Tessenow Architektur studiert und während des Studiums neben architek-

*Pop-Art-Künstler Andy Warhol war öfter in Düsseldorf, sein Siebdruck „Oberkassel 1" zeigt den heutigen Sitz des Unternehmens in der Rheinmetropole —— Pop-art artist Andy Warhol often visited Düsseldorf, and his silkscreen print "Oberkassel 1" depicts the current premises of the company in the Rhine metropolis*

tonischen Großperspektiven auch Zeichnungen unterschiedlichster Stilrichtungen anfertigen müssen. Noch viele Jahre danach holte er sie von Zeit zu Zeit hervor und zeigte sie seinem Sohn.

In den 70er-Jahren überließ Hieronymus Schmitz jungen, oft noch recht unbekannten Künstlern seine Büroräume, in denen dann Ausstellungen stattfanden. „Mein Vater war stets ihr erster und treuester Käufer – jedem kaufte er ein Bild für die Sammlung des Unternehmens ab", berichtet der heutige Geschäftsführer. „Meine bescheidene Aufgabe bei diesen Veranstaltungen beschränkte sich damals auf eine Art kuratorische Assistenz: Vor den Vernissagen half ich immer bei der Hängung der Werke."

## „MIT DEM KUNSTERWERB IST ES SO WIE MIT DEM HAUSKAUF – ES BRAUCHT SEINE ZEIT."

Dieses frühe Heranführen an die Kunst sei sicher ein Grundstein für seine eigene Sammlertätigkeit, erklärt Schmitz. Als er Ende der 70er-Jahre begann, mit seinem eigenen Unternehmen hochwertige Eigentumswohnungen zu bauen, kam er intensiver mit der Kunstszene in Düsseldorf und Umgebung in Berührung: Die Kunstakademie, Besuche in den zahlreichen Galerien der Stadt und Begegnungen mit Künstlern, ob bekannt oder noch unbekannt, schärften sein Kunstverständnis.

Wie sein Vater erwarb auch Ralf Schmitz manches Kunstwerk; und so wuchs die Sammlung aus Malereien, Fotografien und Skulpturen weiter.

„Aber vieles, das habe ich immer wieder feststellen können", sagt er, „lernt man über Kunst und seinen eigenen Kunstgeschmack nicht nur im Umkreis von 100 Kilometern, sondern auf Reisen. Bei jedem unserer Aufenthalte im Ausland besuchen wir Galerien und Museen, um neue Kunst zu entdecken, sie zu erwerben oder eben auch nicht. Bekanntlich sucht sich ein Kunstwerk ja oftmals seinen Sammler aus und nicht umgekehrt – ähnlich wie eine Wohnung ihren Käufer."

---

"All styles are good, except the tiresome kind," French philosopher Voltaire once proclaimed of art. And Ralf Schmitz is inclined to agree. That's not to say he's easily sold on an artwork – far from it. "I'm very choosy and have high standards and so I'm definitely not an impulse buyer. I buy maybe one work per year, sometimes none. It's the same with houses – you have to take your time. And my wife has a veto. If she's doesn't like it, we don't buy it." Art collecting, like house-building, is a family affair for the Kempen-based entrepreneur.

The importance Schmitz attaches to fine art can also be seen in his enthusiasm for the combination of artworks and architecture. He not only collects for personal enjoyment but also considers the needs of the RALF SCHMITZ offices in Kempen, Düsseldorf, Berlin and Hamburg, as well as the requirements of any soon-to-be-completed buildings.

*Haus Bahren in Hamburg (links) und die Düsseldorfer Mercatorterrassen (rechts) nehmen Wappenschmuck und Obelisken mit in*
*die Gegenwart* ——— *Haus Bahren in Hamburg (left) and Düsseldorf's Mercatorterrassen (right) bring blazonry and obelisks into the here and now*

*Die Nachbildung eines neoklassizistischen Bertel-Thorvaldsen-Reliefs empfängt im Berliner Wohnpalais Eisenzahn 1* ——— *A reproduction of a neoclassical*
*Bertel Thorvaldsen relief graces the entrance foyer to our spectacular Eisenzahn 1 development in Berlin*

*Ein riesiges florales Stuckrelief im Stil des Art déco ziert das Foyer des Düsseldorfer Sophienhofs, dessen Interior Oliver Jungel gestaltet hat ——— Art Deco's floral motifs inspired this plaster relief which adorns the Sophienhof foyer in Düsseldorf, designed by Oliver Jungel*

It's thus not uncommon to find photographs, paintings or sculptures hand-picked from the family's own collection in a new development's foyer, staircase or garden. For Schmitz, this symbiosis is key: "I see projects such as Eisenzahn 1, where we decorated the show home with pieces from our collection, as an artistic synthesis." It's a shame, he adds, that one now so rarely finds properties where this once close relationship between art and architecture is maintained. "The norm nowadays is that architects hardly ever want fine art in their buildings because they regard themselves as artists and their completed projects as artworks in their own right."

Schmitz still clearly remembers the first piece of art he bought. It was called Calla and was a colourful, figurative piece by Düsseldorf-based painter Norbert Tadeusz. It wasn't, though, necessarily indicative of the direction his collecting would take. "A whole range of different styles and movements are represented in our collection. Tastes evolve and change over the years. Initially, I was particularly interested in figurative painting; today I'm also fascinated by abstract work."

If you were to look for a recurring theme across the collection, it would be the distinct local bias: there are works by light artist Adolf Luther and Herbert Zangs, a member of the ZERO group, examples of Dieter Krieg's painterly word art, relief-like works by Günther Uecker and monochrome cushion paintings by Gotthard Graubner – most of which have some connection to the Rhineland.

## "ARTWORKS OFTEN FIND THEIR COLLECTOR RATHER THAN THE OTHER WAY ROUND – MUCH LIKE HOMES AND THEIR BUYERS."

It would perhaps be a stretch to suggest that a fine art sensibility has long run in the family. In fact, Ralf Schmitz's father and predecessor as head of the family firm was the first to develop a deep interest in art as well as architecture. Hieronymus Schmitz also had a strong appreciation of different genres and enjoyed passing this on: he studied architecture under the famous designer Heinrich Tessenow and, in addition to large architectural perspectives, also had to produce drawings in various artistic styles during his course. Years later, he would periodically get them out and show them to his son.

In the 1970s, Hieronymus Schmitz allowed young and often little known artists to use his offices and host exhibitions there. "He was always their first and most loyal customer,

*Fassadenmalerei: Der Künstler Reinhart Heinsdorff ließ 1979 für Ralf Schmitz eine abgerissene Kempener Schule meisterlich wiederauferstehen —— Artist Reinhart Heinsdorff resurrected a historic Kempen school at the behest of Ralf Schmitz*

buying a picture from each of them for the firm's collection," says its current managing director. "My own role at such events was reduced to acting as a kind of curatorial assistant – I would always help with the hanging of the artworks."

This early introduction to fine art undoubtedly helped lay the foundations for his own activity as a collector, Schmitz agrees. When he began developing high-quality apartment buildings with his own firm in the late 1970s, he came into contact with the art scene in the Düsseldorf area and honed his appreciation of fine art through visits to the city's Kunstakademie and to its many galleries, as well as through encounters with established and lesser known artists. Like his father before him, Ralf Schmitz became a regular buyer of fine art and so the family collection of paintings, photography and sculptures grew.

"It's not just about what's within a hundred kilometres of your own home though," says Schmitz. "You can also learn a lot about art and your own taste in art through travel. Whenever we go abroad, we seek out galleries and museums in order to discover new art – sometimes we buy something, sometimes we don't. After all, artworks often find their collector rather than the other way round – much like homes and their buyers."

# FACTS & FIGURES: KLOSTERHOF, THE LARGEST PROJECT TO DATE

FOTO RALPH RICHTER    TEXT BETTINA SCHNEUER

Über zehn Jahre lang bemühte sich die Stadt Kempen, Investoren für das zentrale Gelände der ungenutzten, abrissreifen Kreisverwaltung zu finden. Durch dessen Neubebauung sollte die Attraktivität der Kempener Altstadt gesteigert werden. 2010 erhielt – nachdem der Erstinvestor in Konkurs gegangen war – RALF SCHMITZ den Zuschlag. Als Ergebnis einer städtebaulichen Untersuchung errichtete man am Firmenstammsitz ein klassisches Ensemble, das die Umgebung mit einstigem Franziskanerkloster und Paterskirche respektiert: Der Klosterhof gliedert sich in ein größeres Gebäude mit drei Etagen plus Dachgeschoss sowie ein kleineres mit zwei Etagen plus Dachgeschoss. Der Sockel, belegt mit elegantem Naturstein, bietet dem Einzelhandel Platz; darüber gruppieren sich 39 hochwertige Wohnungen um ein südorientiertes Plateau, das einen „Stadtgarten" mit Wandelgang-Pergola entstehen ließ. Die ausgewogene Anlage, eröffnet im Februar 2014, beweist perfekt, wie Tradition und Moderne, Konsum und Wohnkultur harmonieren können.

---

The authorities in Kempen had been seeking investors for the centrally located site, home to a derelict and vacant council building, for more than a decade, hoping its redevelopment would boost the attractiveness of the historic town centre. In 2010, after the initial investor had declared bankruptcy, the contract finally went to RALF SCHMITZ. Having conducted a detailed planning study, the firm came up with a traditionally styled ensemble that would respect the area's architectural heritage, which includes a one-time Franciscan monastery and the Paterskirche church. The resulting Klosterhof development consists of a large building with three full storeys plus a further storey in the roof and a smaller structure with two full storeys plus one in the roof. The ground floor, clad in elegant natural stone, houses retail units; above are 39 high-quality apartments arranged around a south-facing plateau featuring an elevated urban garden with a colonnaded pergola. Opened in February 2014, this finely balanced complex shows just how well high-street shopping and upscale living can mix, while also proving contemporary development can go hand in hand with heritage protection.

RS

GRUNDFLÄCHE
FLOOR AREA
5.500
m²

BAUZEIT
CONSTRUCTION PERIOD
24
Monate / months

UMBAUTER RAUM
BUILT VOLUME
53.000
m³

WOHNUNGEN
APARTMENTS
3.820 m²
39 Einheiten / units

ERDAUSHUB
EXCAVATION

**10.000**
m³

LADENFLÄCHEN
RETAIL SPACE

2.224 m²
8 Einheiten / units

BAUKOSTEN
BUILDING COSTS

**20.000.000**
Euro

HOCHGARTEN
ELEVATED GARDEN

550 Buxus
1.280 Waldsteinia
410 Lavandula

STAHLVERBRAUCH
STEEL USED

**800**
Tonnen / tonnes

TIEFGARAGE
UNDERGROUND PARKING

**173**
Stellplätze / spaces

BETONVERBRAUCH
CONCRETE USED

**20.000**
Tonnen / tonnes

ARCHITEKTEN
ARCHITECTS

**RKW**
Düsseldorf

# REPORT: THE FULL-SERVICE PHILOSOPHY

*Umfassende Betreuung* vom allerersten Interesse über das Kaufen, den *individuellen Ausbau*, den Einzug bis zur Organisation rund ums Wohnen im neuen Zuhause

From *initial consultations* and bespoke fit-outs to handovers and *ongoing maintenance*, RALF SCHMITZ offers expert support every step of the way

FOTOS **RALPH RICHTER, GREGOR HOHENBERG**  TEXT **EVA ZIMMERMANN, PAULINE MEYER**

*Niederlassung Düsseldorf: Während der Beratung kann gleich getestet werden, wie „Tara" und „Madison", die Dornbracht-Klassiker, in der Hand liegen ——— Clients can run the rule over bathroom fittings such as Dornbracht's classic lines*

L uxus ist, genau so zu leben, wie man leben möchte." Programmatischer könnten die Worte eines Geschäftsführers kaum sein. RALF SCHMITZ steht als Marke für Kompromisslosigkeit im Interesse des Kunden – ästhetisch, qualitativ und lokal verwurzelt. Zahllose zufriedene Käufer deutschlandweit hat überzeugt, was funktioniert: Ein mittelständisches und seit 1864 familiengeführtes Unternehmen, das schnell und flexibel agiert und dem selbst gesetzten Höchstanspruch genügt, weil es nur mit ähnlich traditionsreichen Handwerksbetrieben sowie mit renommierten Architekten eng zusammenarbeitet.

„Unsere Kunden stehen nicht auf Prunk, sondern achten auf Stilsicherheit und hochwertigste Materialien", weiß ein Mitarbeiter des Berliner Teams für Akquisition und Verkauf. „Der Baustil spricht eine bestimmte Art von Kunden an, die gebildet und geschmackssicher sind." Um den Vorstellungen der Kunden möglichst genau entsprechen zu können, setzt RALF SCHMITZ auf eine gründliche und aufmerksame Beratung. Wer sich für ein Objekt interessiert, der trifft bereits beim ersten Kontakt auf Mitarbeiter, deren Ziel nicht ein schneller Verkauf ist, sondern absolute Kundenzufriedenheit. Bei der Vermittlung wird nichts übers Knie gebrochen, denn

*Stets gut in Form: Nach dem Einzug ins neue Heim kümmert sich eine kompetente Hausbetreuung um geordnete Abläufe —— Kerb appeal: our expert property management team ensures house and grounds are always well tended and maintained*

die Profis wissen, dass gut Ding auch Weile haben kann: Eine Kundin haderte sechs Jahre lang mit Berlin und entschied sich schließlich doch für eine Wohnung in der Hauptstadt. Bei RALF SCHMITZ konnte sie ihre Traumimmobilie finden.

„Kunden schätzen, dass kein Druck im Verkauf ausgeübt wird, dadurch gewinnt man das Vertrauen", sagt ein Mitarbeiter aus Berlin. Und eine Kundenberaterin aus Düsseldorf ergänzt: „Wenn Paare sich nicht einigen können und dadurch Konflikte entstehen, hilft die Kundenberatung ihnen dabei, eine Entscheidung zu treffen, mit der alle Beteiligten zufrieden sind." Ebenso achten alle Berater auf gut zusammengesetzte, funktionierende Eigentümergemeinschaften, damit auch langfristig alle Beteiligten zufrieden sind. Aus diesem bewusst freundschaftlich gestalteten Kontakt zwischen Kunde und Team entwickelt sich jenes emotionale Band, von dem eine fruchtbare Zusammenarbeit lebt, und genau so will es Ralf Schmitz.

Er selbst arbeitet immer noch hin und wieder im Verkauf, um zu verstehen, was sich seine Kunden wünschen. Gleichzeitig steht er mit seinem Namen dafür, dass am Ende jedes Planungsprozesses ein Unikat in bester Lage entsteht, mit der typischen Handschrift des Unternehmens. Weil viele der Klienten andere SCHMITZ-Immobilien kennen, ist das

Vertrauen in neue Projekte groß. Oft werden schon in der Vorverkaufsphase alle Wohnungen erworben.

Sogenannte Smart-Home-Lösungen, wie sie jetzt in aller Munde sind, nehmen, sagt Geschäftsführer Axel Martin Schmitz, „in der Beurteilung der Immobilien von RALF SCHMITZ keine Kernrolle ein. Eher sind sie ein individuell gewünschtes Add-on, das wir unseren Kunden natürlich immer mit anbieten." Im Fokus stehe vielmehr immer noch die klassische und hochwertige Gebäudeausführung, allerdings unter den Maßgaben hochmodernen Wohnkomforts. So finden sich integrierte Alarmanlagen, Steuerungen mit Bussystem, Fußbodenheizungen und auch hohe Sicherheitsstandards bei Fenstern und Türen.

Die hochwertige Ausstattung beginnt bei den herrschaftlich gestalteten halböffentlichen Bereichen wie Foyer oder Fahrstuhl und reicht in den einzelnen Domizilen von Kaminen über Ankleiden bis zum marmorverkleideten Masterbad.

„Ich fühle mich wie in einem Hotel, wenn ich das Entree und das Treppenhaus betrete. Alles ist so edel, die Materialien sind wunderbar ausgewählt. Ich fühle mich einfach wohl in dieser Atmosphäre", ließ eine Kundin die Mitarbeiter beim Einzug wissen. Genau dieses Gefühl will das Traditionsunternehmen

*Ansehen, anfassen, abwägen, entscheiden: Beratungen zur individuellen Ausstattung basieren auf Kompetenz und Erfahrung* ——— *When it comes to fitting out their new home, buyers profit from the firm's expertise and experience and can inspect possible finishes at first hand*

erzeugen: weniger Opulenz als in der Gründerzeit, doch eine ebenso hochwertige, repräsentative Architektur, die in Würde altert. Am Ende „kann man nur zwischen schön und schön wählen", wie es eine andere Klientin ausdrückte.

Nach Abschluss des Kaufvertrags müssen die Kunden nichts weiter tun, als im Ausstattungskatalog Materialien und Produkte auszuwählen und dann diese Wünsche ihrem Ansprechpartner mitzuteilen. Beiliegende Preislisten sorgen für Transparenz und ermöglichen die Kontrolle etwaiger zusätzlicher Kosten. Um die Gesamtumsetzung und die intensive Abstimmung mit den Baufirmen kümmert sich das Team von RALF SCHMITZ,

das Käufer auch regelmäßig zu Terminen auf der Baustelle einlädt, um Fortschritte zu besichtigen.

Die Wohnungsübergabe gestaltet sich ebenso angenehm. Aufmerksamkeiten in Form von Seifen und Handtüchern begrüßen die Neuankömmlinge, während im Aufnahmeprotokoll notiert wird, was die Kunden noch verändert haben möchten. „In der Gewährleistung ist guter Service besonders wichtig. Weil wir alle nur Menschen sind, kann immer mal ein Fehler passieren, den wir dann beseitigen", sagt eine Mitarbeiterin aus der Düsseldorfer Abteilung Technische Objektbetreuung. Entsprechend positiv sind die Kundenstimmen nach dem Einzug: „Die Zusammenarbeit mit dem Team von RALF SCHMITZ ist wirklich eine Freude: absolut problemlos, aufmerksam, immer lösungsorientiert, sehr kulant und kundenfreundlich."

## „AM ENDE KANN MAN BEI RALF SCHMITZ NUR ZWISCHEN SCHÖN UND SCHÖN WÄHLEN."

„Wir möchten uns ganz herzlich bei Ihnen für Ihre sehr gute und kompetente Arbeit, Beratung und Betreuung bei der Herstellung unserer Wohnung bedanken. Wir sind mit dem Ergebnis sehr zufrieden, dies konnte nur in dieser Zusammenarbeit erzielt werden. Danke!" Auch nach Schlüsselübergabe und Einzug bleibt RALF SCHMITZ rund um die Uhr erreichbar, ob nun bei jemandem ein Einbruch versucht wurde oder sich ein Fenster nicht schließen lässt. Full Service und Qualitätssicherung werden zum untrennbaren Paar: „Für uns ist der langfristige Kontakt mit dem Kunden über die Herstellung der Wohnung hinaus das wichtigste und ehrlichste Feedback. Es ermöglicht uns, stetig besser zu werden,

und bereitet uns die Freude zu erleben, wie wir jemandem ein Zuhause erschaffen können", sagt Ralf Schmitz. Da ist es nur folgerichtig, dass sein Unternehmen auch die technische Objektbetreuung übernimmt, sich als Hausverwaltung um Pflege und Instandhaltung von Haus und Grundstück kümmert, denn nur durch diese Rundumbetreuung lässt sich langfristig aus dem Geschaffenen lernen.

Inzwischen teilt das Unternehmen das Schicksal vieler, die gute Konzepte haben: „Wir werden immer wieder kopiert", sagt eine Mitarbeiterin der Technischen Objektbetreuung aus Kempen. Kompliment mit Wermutstropfen, doch die Klientel weiß Original und Nachahmung zu unterscheiden. Wie es ein Kunde, der über Jahre mehrere Immobilien erwarb, einmal zu Ralf Schmitz sagte: „Wissen Sie, ich hätte so gerne mal bei jemand anderem gekauft – aber es gibt keinen wie Sie!"

———

"Luxury is being able to live exactly how you want to live," says Ralf Schmitz, an assertion that is as clear as it is uncompromising. For himself and his company, not compromising on standards, be it aesthetically or qualitatively, is part and parcel of doing right by the customer – an approach that clearly goes down well, judging by the countless satisfied clients across

*Formenvielfalt: In je originaler Größe präsentiert, erleichtern Modelle dem Kunden die Auswahl seiner neuen Sockelleisten* ——— *A wide range of skirting boards are available; full-sized model pieces help clients choose their preferred height and design*

*SCHMITZ-Dependance Berlin: In stilvoller Umgebung lassen sich Entscheidungen zur Ausstattung der erworbenen Wohnung besser treffen —— RALF SCHMITZ's stylish offices in Berlin: an inspiring setting in which to take decisions affecting the look of that newly acquired home*

Germany who have bought into the RALF SCHMITZ way. In the hands of the same family since its founding in 1864, this traditional firm remains locally rooted, flexible and quick to react, delivering on its promise of perfectionism by working only with renowned architects and skilled contractors similarly committed to traditional values.

## "OUR CLIENTS ARE NOT INTERESTED IN SHOWINESS; THEY WANT CONSUMMATE STYLE AND HIGH-QUALITY MATERIALS."

"Our clients are not interested in showiness; they want consummate style and high-quality materials," maintains a member of the RALF SCHMITZ sales and acquisitions team in Berlin. "Our kind of architecture appeals to a more cultured, discerning type of buyer." To guarantee each client gets exactly the home they want, RALF SCHMITZ sets great store by a thorough and comprehensive consultation process. From the first expression of interest on, potential buyers find themselves dealing with advisers whose aim is not to conclude a quick sale, but to achieve total customer satisfaction. Nothing is ever rushed, buyers are never hurried – after all, Rome wasn't built in a day. One client spent six years deliberating over the decision before finally choosing to buy in Berlin – and finding her dream apartment in a RALF SCHMITZ development.

"Clients appreciate that we don't pressure them during the sales process; that establishes trust," says a staff member from the Berlin office. And an adviser from Düsseldorf adds: "When couples are unable to agree and conflicts arise, we can help them to come to a decision that both parties are comfortable with." RALF SCHMITZ advisers also take into account the need for cohesive, functioning owner communities, thereby ensuring long-term well-being for all concerned. This friendly inter-action between client and team helps to create the emotional ties that are the bedrock of rewarding relationships.

Ralf Schmitz wouldn't have it any other way. In fact, he still sometimes works in sales himself to better understand his clients' requirements. His own good name, after all, gives homebuyers the security that every planned project will develop into a unique prime-location property with all the

*Die RALF-SCHMITZ-Box enthält, jeweils passend zum Stil eines Projekts,
vorausgewählte Fliesen, Böden, Griffe und Armaturen als Anregung* ——
*The SCHMITZ Box contains swatches and samples for tiles, flooring, handles and
taps, all carefully chosen to blend with a new project's aesthetics*

*Zahlreiche Ideen und Ausstattungsoptionen, eine feine Materialauslese und umfassende Baubetreuung fügen sich zum individuellen Interieur —— Diverse options and suggestions, carefully selected materials and full-service support help each client put together their own personal home*

firm's trademark qualities. Many would-be buyers are already familiar with other SCHMITZ properties and, as a result, have great confidence when it comes to the firm's new developments, in which units often sell out in advance.

The much-discussed issue of smart home technology, meanwhile, is "not a key factor when considering a RALF SCHMITZ property," says co-director Axel Schmitz, "more like an individual add-on that we of course offer to all our clients." Instead, the focus is still very much on the traditional, high-quality build and on combining that with state-of-the-art comfort and convenience. New developments feature built-in alarms, electronic control systems, underfloor heating and highly secure doors and windows.

The fit-out, too, is of the very highest quality, as seen in everything from communal areas such as foyers and lifts to the fireplaces, dressing rooms and marble-clad master bathrooms of the individual residences. "As soon as I walk into the hall or staircase, I feel like I'm in a hotel," one client said upon moving in. "Everything is so luxurious," she went on, "the materials are beautifully chosen. It's an environment I just feel really at home in." Such sentiments are exactly what RALF SCHMITZ

wants to deliver – via properties that, while less opulent than their late-19-century forebears, boast similarly high-quality architecture and a look that ages well. Or as another client puts it: "The only dilemma is which of the beautiful homes to choose."

## "AS SOON AS I WALK INTO THE ENTRANCE HALL OR STAIRCASE, I FEEL LIKE I'M IN A HOTEL."

After the contract is signed, all homebuyers have to do is select materials and products from the fittings catalogue and inform their adviser what they have chosen. The enclosed price lists mean there is transparency right from the start and make additional costs easier to manage. Buyers can then sit back and let RALF SCHMITZ take care of implementing those choices and liaising with construction firms, though they also have regular opportunities to visit the site.

Handover is similarly hassle-free. Thoughtful touches such as soaps and towels make for a warm welcome, while the handover protocol documents any changes the clients might request. "Good customer service is particularly important when it comes to the warranty. Mistakes can occasionally happen – we are all only human – and will be rectified," says a member of the marketing team in Düsseldorf. This is reflected in the positive feedback the company receives from clients after they've moved in: "The team at RALF SCHMITZ is an absolute pleasure to work with: thoroughly uncomplicated and always friendly, focused on finding solutions, very accommodating and customer-friendly."

"We would like to say a big thank-you for your outstanding and expert work, advice and service in developing our apartment. We are very happy with the results which could only have been achieved by working together. Thank you!" Even after buyers have taken receipt of their home and moved in, the firm remains at their service around the clock, whether they discover an attempted break-in or find a window won't close. For RALF SCHMITZ, full service and quality assurance

are indivisible: "For us, maintaining long-term contact with our clients beyond the initial development is the most important and honest way of getting feedback. It allows us to keep on improving and gives us the pleasure of seeing how what we have created becomes someone's home," says Ralf Schmitz. It's only logical then that the firm should look after the upkeep and maintenance of building and grounds  via its own property management services; after all, only such a full-service approach enables it to gain long-term insights into its built work.

As is so often the case with good ideas, it's an approach that has spawned imitators. "Others keep copying us," says a member of the property management team in Kempen. While this may be a compliment the company could do without, it's gratifying to know that customers can still distinguish between the original and mimics. As one client who has bought a number of the firm's properties over the years once said to Ralf Schmitz: "You know, I would've really liked to buy from someone else this time – but there's no one that compares to you!"

*Fundierte Informationen für Kaufinteressierte: Zu jedem neuen Berliner Projekt gibt es aufwendig gestaltete Unterlagen ——— In-depth information for potential buyers: every new Berlin development is accompanied by beautifully designed sales literature*

# AT A GLANCE: BATHROOMS

FEINE OBERFLÄCHEN AUS DIVERSEN NATURSTEINEN UND
HOCHWERTIGSTE AUSSTATTUNGSELEMENTE BEKANNTER HERSTELLER
VEREDELN DEN START UND DAS ENDE EINES JEDEN TAGES

FINE STONE FINISHES PLUS FIRST-CLASS FIXTURES AND
FITTINGS BY RENOWNED MANUFACTURERS ADD LUXURY TO THE
BEGINNING AND END OF EACH DAY

BERLIN, HAUS WEYHE

*First class: Baden mit Blick in den
eigenen Garten, gerahmt von Marmor
in warmen erdigen Nuancen (2013)*

*First-class surroundings: the private
garden view is elegantly framed by
marble in warm earth shades (2013)*

DÜSSELDORF, LINDENSTRASSE

*Grandezza: Grauer und schwarzer Marmor
umkleiden die Walk-in-Dusche und den
opulenten Waschtisch im Masterbad (2012)*

*Grey and black marble surfaces lend a refined
look to the master bathroom's opulent
washstand and walk-in shower (2012)*

DÜSSELDORF, MALKASTENSTRASSE

*Opulentes Baudenkmal: eine Badoase mit
Crema Marfil, Nero Marquina, Wanne von
Bette und Dornbracht-Armaturen (2006)*

*Bathroom as opulent oasis – with
Crema Marfil, Nero Marquina, Bette tub
and Dornbracht taps (2006)*

BERLIN, GOLDFINKWEG 40

*Dramatik: Dunkler Pietra Grigia im
Großformat umhüllt die Dusche mit
raffiniert eingelassener Ablage (2014)*

*Large tiles of dark Pietra Grigia and
a clever inset shelf make for
a dramatic-looking shower (2014)*

**BERLIN, GRIEGSTRASSE**

*Brillanz: Im Grunewalder Stadthaus schmückt Deckenstuck sogar das Bad, das zur Ankleide hinüberleitet (2012)*

*Even the bathroom, which opens onto the dressing room, has ceiling mouldings at this Grunewald townhouse (2012)*

**KEMPEN, KLOSTERSTRASSE**

*Kunstsalon: Die Wanne von Traditional Bathrooms flankieren in Halbsäulen Motive der Tapete „Early Views of India" von de Gournay (2013)*

*Scenic backdrop: half column-framed sheets of de Gournay's "Early Views of India" wallpaper flank a Traditional Bathrooms tub (2013)*

**DÜSSELDORF, HAUS BATTENBERG**

*Glanz: Eine Sauna vervollkommnet den Wellnessfaktor des lichten Bades mit Waschtisch und Wannenumrandung aus Silestone Haiku Leather (2013)*

*A sauna ups the wellness factor in this airy bathroom, which has a washstand and bath rim of Silestone Haiku Leather (2013)*

**BERLIN, PETER-LENNÉ-STRASSE**

*Duett: maßgefertigter Marmorwaschtisch mit großzügiger Handtuchablage in einer klassizistischen Dahlemer Stadtvilla (2013)*

*Bespoke side-by-side marble basins with a lavish towel shelf grace this classically styled Dahlem villa (2013)*

**HAMBURG, ROOSENS WEG**

*Finesse: Fast fugenlos fügen sich die Natursteinwände und das grazile Waschbecken zusammen (2014)*

*Here, stone-clad walls and a sleek washstand form an almost seamless ensemble (2014)*

# ICONIC
# URBAN VILLAS

SIE VERKÖRPERN *BAUKULTUR* , STIL
UND GESCHICHTE: STADTHÄUSER SIND
BAUWERKE *FÜR GENERATIONEN*

---

EMBODYING *BUILDING CULTURE*,
STYLE AND TRADITION, THESE ELEGANT
HOMES ARE *BUILT TO LAST*

FOTOS **GREGOR HOHENBERG, RALPH RICHTER**   TEXT **INA MARIE KÜHNAST**

*Griegstraße, Berlin-Grunewald: Luft, Licht und
Grün – Villenkultur par excellence. Traditionelle
Architekturelemente wie die bodentiefen Fenster
und eine vorgelagerte, klug getreppte Terrasse
heben geschmackvoll vergangene Zeiten ins Jetzt*

---

*Griegstrasse, Berlin-Grunewald: light, leafy
and airy, this fabulous take on the traditional villa
tastefully updates classic details such as floor-
to-ceiling windows and a neatly stepped terrace*

*Schöne Schwestern, raffinierte Zugangsloggien:*
*Nahe dem Rhein entstanden die zwei*
*Stadthäuser mit rückwärtigen Privatgärten*

*Our delightful twin townhouses close*
*to the Rhine boast elegant front porches and*
*private back gardens*

# CARMENSTRASSE
*Düsseldorf-Oberkassel*

Hinter dem noblen Hauptbau liegen zwei
charmante Gartenvillen mit eigenen Grundstücken,
in denen sich pulsierendes Großstadtleben und
stille Naturverbundenheit perfekt vereinen lassen

Situated behind the handsome main building are
a pair of enchanting villas set in their
own individual grounds – private sanctuaries that
combine city living and leafy surroundings

# KENTENICH HOF
## Gerhard-Domagk-Straße,
## Düsseldorf-Golzheim

# RICHARD-STRAUSS-STRASSE
*Berlin-Grunewald*

*Gediegene Townhouses: Aufgang, Säulen,
bodentiefe Fenster und stille Gärten
zitieren den Charme britischer Stadthäuser*

*Class act: the entrance steps, Ionic
columns and deep windows echo genteel
English townhouses*

Die herrschaftlichen Fassaden der beiden
hochwertigen Stadthäuser vereinen gekonnt
historische und zeitgenössische Stildetails

*The handsome façades of these two
high-end townhouses skilfully blend classical
and contemporary details*

# GRIEGSTRASSE
*Berlin-Grunewald*

# DAHLEM DUO
## *Gelfertstraße, Berlin*

*Im Nobelviertel entsteht diese kultivierte Anlage:
Lebensart mitten im Grünen, dennoch zentral*

*Under construction: this refined
ensemble offers leafy living in the heart of
one of Berlin's best neighbourhoods*

# LEOSTRASSE

*Düsseldorf-Oberkassel*

*Bereits 2005 entstanden in dieser Toplage
sechs charmante Stadthäuser, deren Portale und
Giebel sich subtil unterscheiden – ähnlich wie
bei ihren zeitlos schönen Londoner Vorbildern*

*Like London's finest terraces, the six charming
townhouses built in 2005 in a prime
location boast subtle variations in their porticos
and frontages*

Meine Kindheit war gehegt und glücklich. Mit vier Geschwistern wuchs ich auf in einem eleganten Stadthaus, das mein Vater sich und den Seinen erbaut hatte (...)." Es braucht nicht viel Fantasie, um sich das großbürgerliche Leben der Familie von Thomas Mann in jener schmucken hanseatischen Kaufmannsvilla inmitten der Lübecker Altstadt vorzustellen, die heute als das Buddenbrookhaus fast so weltbekannt ist wie der Schriftsteller.

Ein Haus, wie Thomas Mann es beschrieb, ist jedoch nicht nur bloßes Bauwerk – sondern vor allem ein Zuhause. Durch seine Räumlichkeiten zu schreiten ist, als blättere man in einem Album aus persönlichen Erinnerungen und Geschichten. Architekturen wie die für Stadthäuser, bereits seit dem Barock bekannt, stehen nie still, denn die Generationen hauchen den Gebäuden stets neues, individuelles Leben ein und passen sie den jeweiligen persönlichen Ansprüchen an. Ab dem 19. Jahrhundert ließen sich wohlhabende Familien Häuser zunächst in Vororten oder in eher ländlicher Lage errichten – hier lebten sie in eleganten Bauten mit eindrucksvollen Fassaden und parkähnlichen Gärten. Idyllisch inszenierte Blickachsen aus den repräsentativen Räumlichkeiten im Hochparterre hinaus in das umgebende Grün standen seit jeher für den besonderen Charme dieser herrschaftlichen, großbürgerlichen Wohnform.

Bis heute tüfteln Architekten und Landschaftsgärtner an der perfekten Harmonie aus Architektur und Gartenkultur. Daher finden sich sorgfältig geplante Grünanlagen zusammen mit traditionellen Fassadenelementen wie Portikus, Säulen oder Erkern auch in der zeitgenössischen Architektur als gelungene Symbiose wieder: Die Berliner Stadthäuser von RALF SCHMITZ in der Grunewalder Griegstraße oder das Premiumprojekt Dahlem Duo in der Gelfertstraße sind noble Belege dafür. Auch klassizistische Architekturen wie im Düsseldorfer Projekt Crescent Gardens, wo sich fünf britisch anmutende Stadthäuser im sanften Bogen um einen privaten *pocket park* legen, zeigen, wie stark traditionelle Formen immer noch zu uns sprechen und wie gut wir uns in diesen Bauwerken aufgehoben fühlen.

Ganz im Sinne des antiken Architekturtheoretikers Vitruv (1. Jahrhundert v. Chr.) vereinen sich „Festigkeit, Nützlichkeit und Schönheit" bis heute noch in der Vorstellung von harmonischer Architektur – selbst im stetigen Wandel des 21. Jahrhunderts hat sich dieses Konzept kaum verändert. Wer heutzutage die Nähe zur Stadt nicht missen und trotzdem viel Wohn- und Gartenfläche nutzen möchte, dem bietet die *urban villa* einen idealen Lebensstil. Städtisch und doch ruhig gelegen, vereint sie Vorzüge des urbanen Umfelds mit der Ruhe eines ländlich gelegenen, großen Hauses und eignet sich je nach Größe als Familienheim oder auch als Domizil für ein Paar, das in seinem Stadthaus nicht nur leben, sondern hier auch das Arbeiten integrieren möchte.

Klassisch und zeitlos, hochmodern und kompromisslos komfortabel – Thomas Mann hätte große Freude an den Stadthäusern von RALF SCHMITZ gehabt.

---

"My childhood was sheltered and happy," wrote Thomas Mann of his early life. "We five brothers and sisters grew up in an elegant townhouse, built by my father for himself and his loved ones (...)." It's easy to imagine the upbringing he enjoyed in the handsome merchant's house in the heart of old Lübeck, a building that now functions as the Buddenbrookhaus museum and is almost as famous as Mann himself.

A townhouse like this is not just a house though – it is, first and foremost, a home. Wandering around its rooms is like browsing through an album of personal memories and stories. With both townhouses and villas however, architecture doesn't stand still; new generations put their own stamp on them, tailoring the design to their personal needs.

In the 19th century, a great many well-off families built themselves villas in suburban or out-of-town locations. Park-like gardens, impressive façades and grand ground-floor reception rooms with fabulous sight lines towards the surrounding greenery were the defining features of these residences, features that have influenced this upmarket dwelling type ever since. Today, architects and landscape designers continue to strive for the perfect synthesis between home and garden, blending carefully planned outdoor spaces with traditional façade details. Urban villas in Berlin such as RALF SCHMITZ's Griegstrasse properties in Grunewald or our premium Dahlem Duo development are first-class examples of this contemporary interpretation of the genre, as well as our Crescent Gardens project in Düsseldorf, where a terrace of five English-style townhouses gently arcs around a private pocket park – proof of how traditional architectural forms continue to appeal, and how at home we still feel in their midst. Durability, utility and beauty, as expounded by the Roman architectural theorist Vitruvius, still define what architecture should be and remain highly prized even today. For those seeking spacious accommodation and generous gardens in the city, our urban villas are ideal. Thomas Mann would surely have approved of these refined residences.

# RUBENSSTRASSE
## *Düsseldorf-Zoo*

*In exklusiver Lage wachsen fünf stilvolle
Stadthäuser aus Backstein mit dem
Flair flandrischer Bautradition empor*

*Coming soon to exclusive Zooviertel, our
quintet of chic, brick-clad homes
nods to the charming Flemish style*

# CRESCENT GARDENS
## *Sybelstraße, Düsseldorf-Zoo*

*Eine reduziert-moderne und
gelungene Interpretation der
typisch englischen Reihenhäuser*

*These understated townhouses
offer a contemporary take on London's
Regency terraces*

# NACHWORT

Architektur ist kein kurzlebiger Modeartikel. Gute Architektur nutzt sich nicht ab. Sie ist zeitlos schön, weil sie auf eine klassische Formensprache zurückgreift, die sich über Jahrhunderte bewährt hat und auch künftig überdauern wird. Als familiengeführtes Unternehmen, das auf seine vor über 150 Jahren begründete Baukultur stolz ist, steht RALF SCHMITZ für Werte wie Beständigkeit und Erfahrung – gepaart mit dem Streben nach Fortschritt und Perfektion.

Als Projektentwickler, der sich auf besonders hochwertige Wohnimmobilien an vier Standorten spezialisiert hat, setzen wir auf den Spannungsbogen Alt – Neu. Die Entwürfe für unsere Stadtvillen und Stadthäuser schöpfen ihre Inspiration aus Europas geschätztem großbürgerlichem Wohnrepertoire: typisch britische *terraced houses*, charmante flämische Grachtenhäuser ebenso wie noble Pariser Apartmentbauten und die imposanten Jugendstil- und Gründerzeitgebäude deutscher Metropolen. Auch unsere durchdachten Grundrisse nehmen auf, was seit jeher für Großzügigkeit und Stil steht – etwa hohe Decken, Flügeltüren, bodentiefe Fenster, Gipsstuck und Eichenparkett. Im Inneren setzen wir zudem auf jenen gehobenen Komfort von heute, den raffinierte Bäder, klug an die Wohnräume angebundene Küchen und natürlich eine hochmoderne Haustechnik garantieren. Diese Verknüpfung schätzen Selbstnutzer ebenso wie Anleger, in deren Fokus der deutsche Immobilienmarkt zunehmend rückt.

Für unsere Projekte beauftragen wir nur renommierte Architekten, die wie wir Traditionen respektieren. Deren Planungen setzt die firmeneigene technische Abteilung mit vielen, sehr erfahrenen Bauingenieuren in erstklassige Bauqualität um. Dazu kommen einzigartige, deutschlandexklusive Kooperationen, zum Beispiel mit dem italienischen Luxuslabel Bottega Veneta sowie dem Pariser Gartendesigner Louis Benech für zwei sehr repräsentative Berliner Bauvorhaben. Ein solch stimmiges Gesamtkonzept unterscheidet RALF SCHMITZ deutlich von Wettbewerbern und Nachahmern. Das nehmen auch unsere Kunden wahr: Ihre Ansprüche an Architektur und Ausstattung der Projekte sind gestiegen und steigen weiter, denn sie sind stilsicher, gebildet und kennen das, was international – ob in New York, London oder Paris – *state of the art* ist. Da RALF SCHMITZ sich auf relativ kleine Projekte in einem gewachsenen und hochattraktiven Umfeld konzentriert, kann jeder Erwerber individuell betreut und auf seine Wünsche weitestgehend eingegangen werden; dafür sorgt eine eigene Abteilung für Kundenbetreuung.

Mit unserer etablierten Mischung aus Tradition und Weitsicht planen wir aktuell einerseits neue Projekte an allen Standorten, darunter so spektakuläre wie das am Berliner Ludwigkirchplatz, an der Graf-Recke-Straße im Düsseldorfer Zooviertel oder die reizvollen Stadthäuser in Hamburg-Nienstedten. Andererseits geht nahtlos und erfolgreich die Verantwortung von der vierten auf die fünfte Generation über: Mit der gleichen Leidenschaft wie die Generationen davor und ausgerüstet mit einer erstklassigen Ausbildung wird sie das Unternehmen familienbestimmt in die Zukunft führen und seine Position als führender Entwickler von Premiumimmobilien in Deutschland sichern.

Ralf Schmitz
*Kempen, im Dezember 2017*

# EPILOGUE

Architecture is no short-lived fashion trend. And good architecture doesn't ever get worn out. It is timelessly beautiful because it draws on classic aesthetics that have proven themselves over the centuries and will continue to shine through the future. As a family firm that is proud of the 150 years of architectural culture it has built, RALF SCHIMTZ stands for values such as reliability and experience – which we pair with the pursuit of progress and perfection.

Specialised in particularly high-quality residential real estate in four locations, RALF SCHMITZ places great weight upon the balance of old and new. The designs for our urban villas and multifamily homes draw their inspiration from Europe's repertoire of patrician living: typical British terraced houses, charming Flemish canal homes as well as elegant Parisian apartments buildings and the stately Art Nouveau and Wilhelminian apartments of German cities. Our thoughtful floor plans encompass elements that have come to embody grandeur and style: high ceilings, double doors, floor-length windows, decorative stucco, and oak parquet flooring. Our interiors place a high value upon upscale modern comforts, such as sophisticated bathrooms, kitchens smartly adjoined to living spaces and of course state-of-the-art home utilities and appliances. Residents appreciate this combination, as do investors, who have recently turned their attention to the German real estate market.

For our projects, we only commission renowned architects who respect tradition as much as we do, and our in-house technical division of very experienced engineers translates these plans into first-class structures. Then there are our unique collaborations, exclusive in Germany, such as with the Italian luxury label Bottega Veneta and the Parisian garden designer Louis Benech for two prestigious projects in Berlin. This kind of comprehensive concept distinguishes RALF SCHMITZ from its competitors and imitators. And our clients have sensed this; their expectations of the projects' architecture and interior design have risen and continue to rise, for they are stylistically confident, educated and share an international understanding – from New York, London or Paris – of what it means to live in a state-of-the-art home. Because RALF SCHMITZ concentrates on relatively small projects in an established and highly attractive environment, our client management department can individually consult with every buyer to fulfill as many wishes as possible.

We are currently planning new buildings with our established blend of tradition and vision in all our locations, including spectacular projects in Berlin near Ludwigkirchplatz, on Graf-Recke-Strasse in Düsseldorf-Zoo or the appealing urban villas in Hamburg-Nienstedten. At the same time, responsibility for the firm is transitioning seamlessly and successfully from the fourth to the fifth generation. With the same passion as the previous generations and armed with first-class training, the newest generation  is poised to guide the family firm into the future and to secure its position as leading developer for premium real estate in Germany.

Ralf Schmitz
*Kempen, December 2017*

# CREDITS

ABTEI MARIENDONK, NIEDERFELD BEI GREFRATH  29
BILDARCHIV DER STADT KEMPEN  29, 30, 31
EBERLE, TODD, NEW YORK  COVER, 10/11, 12, 13, 14, 15, 16, 18/19, 90, 91, 101, 108, 116, 117, 126, 154, 155, 162
50 JAHRE PRIVATBAUMEISTER. 1880 – 1930, FESTSCHRIFT FÜR ANDREAS SCHMITZ UND DIE FIRMA
P. H. SCHMITZ & CIE, GREFRATH BEI KREFELD O. J. (1930)  31
FRIESE, JAN, BERLIN  148
HATZIUS, ACHIM, BERLIN  151
HEISSNER, OLIVER, HAMBURG  45, 60, 99, 120, 127, 138, 142
HEMPEL, JÖRG, AACHEN  61, 92/93, 100, 127
100 JAHRE IM BAUGESCHEHEN AM NIEDERRHEIN, HRSGG. VON DER FIRMA HEINRICH SCHMITZ KG,
KEMPEN O. J. (1964)  31
HOHENBERG, GREGOR, BERLIN  14, 20, 21, 22, 23, 24, 25, 27, 33, 60, 62, 67, 71, 75, 76, 78, 81, 86, 98, 126,
128, 130, 131,132/133, 134, 141, 146, 149, 150, 152, 154, 155, 158, 163, 166
HUTHMACHER, WERNER, BERLIN  26, 27, 94, 101, 118, 126, 160
MOUSSAVI, MAJID, DÜSSELDORF  102, 103, 104, 105, 106, 107
NOSHE, BERLIN  COVER, 26, 31, 34, 36, 38/39, 40, 41, 42, 43, 44, 45, 46, 48, 49, 50, 51, 52, 55, 56, 57, 58, 59,
60, 61, 90, 96/97, 99, 100, 110/111, 112, 113, 114, 115, 126, 127, 141, 147, 154, 155, 156, 164
MÜLLER, STEFAN, BERLIN  85
SZCZEPANIAK, OLAF, HAMBURG  121
SCHMITZ, RALF, KEMPEN, UNTERNEHMENSCHRONIK DER RALF SCHMITZ WOHNUNGSBAUGESELLSCHAFT
1977-2000, 4 BDE. P.  143
RALF SCHMITZ GMBH & CO. KGAA, KEMPEN  28, 31, 139
RICHTER, RALPH, DÜSSELDORF  COVER, 26, 44, 61, 73, 82, 83, 84, 87, 88, 100, 134, 136, 144/145, 159, 167
TREESE, SEBASTIAN, BERLIN  COVER, 8, 68, 70, 72, 74, 76, 78, 80, 123, 124, 125
WYST, ANDRÉ M., BERLIN  32, 100, 153

BRAUN, MATTI, UNTITLED, 2013  38
HÖDICKE, K. H., DOPPELKOPF II, 1989  83
GRAUBNER, GOTTHARD, HAUT STYLIT, 1965  12
LINSSEN, JUPP, TRIPTYCHON, 2008  120
SIEM, WIEBKE, O. T. (AUGE), 2007  83
TOMÁS SARACENO, AIRPORT CITY, CLOUD CITY 6 CLOUD MODULES, 2013  38/39, 113
UECKER, GÜNTHER STURZ DES KÜNSTLERISCHEN GENIUS (FÜR JOSEPH BEUYS), 1986  83
WAKULTSCHIK, MAXIM, MULTI-PERSONALITY  102
WAKULTSCHIK, MAXIM, TDC WOOD  104
WARHOL, ANDY, OBERKASSEL 1, 1981  140

# IMPRINT

**PUBLISHER**  RALF SCHMITZ GMBH & CO. KGaA
**CONCEPT, ART DIRECTION, DESIGN**  ANDRÉ M. WYST
**CONCEPT, EDITOR IN CHIEF**  BETTINA SCHNEUER

**TEXT**  INA MARIE KÜHNAST, PAULINE MEYER, HOLGER REINERS, RALF SCHMITZ, BETTINA SCHNEUER, CHRISTIAN TRÖSTER, EVA ZIMMERMANN
**TRANSLATION**  RACHEL MARKS-RITZENHOFF, IAIN REYNOLDS, LUISA WEISS

**PHOTO**  TODD EBERLE, JAN FRIESE, ANDREAS GEHRKE/NOSHE, ACHIM HATZIUS, OLIVER HEISSNER, JÖRG HEMPEL, GREGOR HOHENBERG, WERNER HUTHMACHER, MAJID MOUSSAVI, STEFAN MÜLLER, OLAF SZCZEPANIAK, RALPH RICHTER, SEBASTIAN TREESE, ANDRÉ M. WYST
**COPY EDITING**  DR. MARKUS WEBER


**STAMMSITZ KEMPEN**
RALF SCHMITZ GMBH & CO. KGaA
MOORENRING 29
47906 KEMPEN
TEL 02152 9177-0
KEMPEN@RALFSCHMITZ.COM

**DÜSSELDORF**
RALF SCHMITZ GMBH & CO. KGaA
KAISER-FRIEDRICH-RING 1
40545 DÜSSELDORF
TEL 0211 447267-0
DUESSELDORF@RALFSCHMITZ.COM

**BERLIN**
RALF SCHMITZ GMBH & CO. KGaA
KURFÜRSTENDAMM 58
10707 BERLIN
TEL 030 3180596-0
BERLIN@RALFSCHMITZ.COM

**HAMBURG**
RALF SCHMITZ GMBH & CO. KGaA
NEUER WALL 34
20354 HAMBURG
TEL 040 3060597-0
HAMBURG@RALFSCHMITZ.COM

WWW.RALFSCHMITZ.COM

RS

RALF SCHMITZ

© 2018 Ralf Schmitz GmbH & Co. KGaA.
© 2018 teNeues Media GmbH & Co. KG, Kempen
All rights reserved.

Proofreading by Dr Suzanne Kirkbright, Artes Translations (English)
and Stephanie Rebel, teNeues Media (German)
Editorial coordination by Pit Pauen, teNeues Media
Production by Sandra Jansen, teNeues Media

ISBN 978-3-96171-095-9

Library of Congress Number: 2017958242
Printed in the Czech Republic
Picture and text rights reserved for all countries. No part of this
publication may be reproduced in any manner whatsoever.

While we strive for utmost precision in every detail,
we cannot be held responsible for any inaccuracies, neither for
any subsequent loss or damage arising.
Every effort has been made by the publisher to contact
holders of copyright to obtain permission to reproduce copyrighted
material. However, if any permissions have been inadvertently
overlooked, teNeues Publishing Group will be pleased to
make the necessary and reasonable arrangements at the first
opportunity. Bibliographic information published by the Deutsche
Nationalbibliothek.

The Deutsche Nationalbibliothek lists this publication in the
Deutsche Nationalbibliografie; detailed bibliographic data are
available on the Internet at http://dnb.dnb.de.

Published by teNeues Publishing Group

teNeues Media GmbH & Co. KG
Am Selder 37, 47906 Kempen, Germany
Phone: +49-(0)2152-916-0, Fax: +49-(0)2152-916-111
e-mail: books@teneues.com

Press department: Andrea Rehn
Phone: +49-(0)2152-916-202
e-mail: arehn@teneues.com

Munich Office
Pilotystraße 4, 80538 Munich, Germany
Phone: +49-(0)89-443-8889-62
e-mail: bkellner@teneues.com

Berlin Office
Kohlfurter Straße 41–43, 10999 Berlin, Germany
Phone: +49-(0)30-4195-3526-23
e-mail: ajasper@teneues.com

teNeues Publishing Company
350 7th Avenue, Suite 301, New York, NY 10001, USA
Phone: +1-212-627-9090, Fax: +1-212-627-9511

teNeues Publishing UK Ltd.
12 Ferndene Road, London SE24 0AQ, UK
Phone: +44-(0)20-3542-8997

teNeues France S.A.R.L.
39, rue des Billets, 18250 Henrichemont, France
Phone: +33-(0)2-4826-9348, Fax: +33-(0)1-7072-3482

www.teneues.com

**teNeues Publishing Group**
Kempen
Berlin
London
Munich
New York
Paris

**teNeues**